STRATEGIC FINANCIAL MANAGEMENT
PRINCIPLES AND APPLICATIONS

BY BEN BOLFA

INTRODUCTION

This study material is prepared for learners who do most of their studies on their own. The structure of the study unit is quite different from the conventional text book writing. Ben Bolfa has made much effort in putting the book rich and easy to understand. However, the learners need to do more extra reading in order to enrich their knowledge on the course.

The learners are expected to make the best use of library facilities and internet services. The references are provided to guide and direct the learners in the selection of reading materials required.

HOW TO STUDY THE UNITS

You are welcome to the study units. The study units are classified under modules. The breaking down of the units into modules is to make the reader understand everything under each module.

It is expected that the learner should devote at least 6 to 8 hours to complete a module.

PRACTICAL EXERCISES AND TESTS

There are two key points to note here. The self- assessment exercises (SAES) and tutor- marked assignments (TMA). The self- assessment exercises are provided at the end of each module. The exercise will assess how far you have understood the units under such a module. Solutions are provided at the end of the study to help you assess yourself how well you have understood the study.

The Tutor- marked assessment is provided at the end of the study. It is in form of examination for you to answer and send to the study center for your continuous assessment (CA).

The study center wish success as you undertake the study of each unit under each module.

CONTENTS   PAGE

MODULE 1

UNIT 1   NATURE, SCOPE AND PURPOSE OF FINANCIAL MANAGEMENT

CONTENTS

1.0   Introduction
2.0   Objectives
3.0   Main Content
    3.1   Financial Management
    3.2   Objectives of Financial Management
    3.3   Functions of the Financial Managers/Roles of Financial Management
4.0   Conclusion
5.0   Summary
6.0   Tutor-Marked Assignment

1.0   INTRODUCTION

In this unit, we will attempt to explain the nature of financial management. The unit also examines the objectives of financial management. It also explores the functions of the financial manager/roles of financial management.

2.0   OBJECTIVES

At the end of the unit, you should be able to:

- define financial management
- state the objectives of financial management
- describe the functions of the financial manager/roles of financial management.

3.0   Main Content

3.1   Financial Management

Financial Management is that part of management which is concerned mainly with raising funds in the most economic and suitable manner; using these funds as profitably (for a given risk level) as possible; planning future operations, and controlling current performance and future developments through financial accounting, budgeting, statistical analysis and other means

In other words, financial management is the process of planning and controlling of the financial resources of a firm. It includes the acquisition, allocation and management of firms' financial resources. It is concerned with how best to manage an organization's resources in order to make sure that the resources are maximized fully.

The finance functions in all their facets are concerned with decisions about investment, financing and appropriation of profit. The quality of decision taken in these aspects – investment, financing and profit distribution has a lot of implications for the success of a business.

The types of questions that financial management seeks to answer are as follows:

i.   What percentage of funds needed by a business should be obtained from outsiders and what percentage from the owners?

ii.   The bank keeps offering us new types of business loans, but we like the traditional old arrangement, should we change?

iii.   Is it worthwhile for the company to replace its existing manufacturing machines with a new computer integrated system?

iv.   The earning per share (EPS) figure for the company is falling despite the fact the manufacturing facilities have been modernized, should one be considered?

v.   A potential customer has enquired whether we will sell goods to him now, and allows him 6 months to pay. Is it profitable to do so?

vi.   What percentage of the annual profit should be paid out to shareholders as dividends?

3.2   Objectives of Financial Management

The major objective of management is to maximize the shareholders' wealth. The shareholders' wealth is the present value of future cash flows or present value of future dividends payable to the shareholders infinitely.

The Shareholders wealth maximization is gradually becoming the single and narrow objective of firms pursued by financial managers making it the most fashionable objective of the firm.

This is being achieved through a combination of goals such as:

i.   Increase in the market share of the firm
ii.   Increase in reported profits
iii.   Continuous survival of the business
iv.   Provision of valued services to customers
v.   Ensuring public acceptability of the firm and its products/services coupled with both social acceptability and legal acceptability.

3.3   Functions of the Financial Manager/Roles of Financial Management

i.   **Financial Decision:** This is the effective management of the capital structure of the business. The financial manager must ensure maximum mixture of debt and equity in financing the firm, so as to ensure maximum returns to the shareholders the maximum mix of finance of debt and equity must be established to maximize the returns of shareholders.

ii.   **Investment Decision:** This involves the identification of viable projects. The financial manager should select the most profitable investment portfolio that will reduce to the barest minimum the risk of the organization not maximizing stockholders' wealth.

iii.   **Dividend Decision:** This involves the determination of the appropriate amount to be paid as dividend and the profit that would be ploughed back to finance expansion in the company. The financial manager must select the best dividend policy per time, the timing dividend, the forms of dividend to be paid, the methods of payment, the amount to be paid etc. The fund(s) to use is an important factor to be considered by the financial Manager. As dividend can be paid either in cash (cash dividend), or by share allocation (stock dividend).

The amount to be retained by the firm for future finances must also be considered. Since retained earnings is the cheapest source of fund to the firm, and a bird in hand is worth more than ten in the bush. Thus, cash dividend will mean more to some section/segment of investors than the retained earnings which still remains an integral part of the shareholder's wealth. Thus, the financial manager must be able to draw the border line between amount to be declared as well as retained for future use.

iv.   **Acquisition Decision:** The financial manager must be interested in the organizations internal and external growth. The growth of corporate organization can be varied, either by way of merger or acquisition, by backward integration or forward integration etc.

v.   **Working Capital Management (Treasury Management):** It is the totality of management of cash, debtor prepayments, stocks creditors, short term loans accruals, etc. to ensure the profitability of the firm's operation. It is the management of current asset and liabilities of firm, which is fast becoming important in the face of high cost of capital. In modern financial world, efficient management of the working capital will ensure maximum utilization of scarce financial resource and ipso facto maximization of the shareholder's wealth.

vi.   **Financial Control and Reporting:** Financial control and reporting is an important function of the financial manager. He must be able to present a lucid yet concise financial report that provides management with required information necessary to take financial decision.

4.0 CONCLUSION

In this unit, we examined the definitions of financial management. We also outlined the major functions and roles of financial management in an organization as well as the objectives of financial management.

5.0 SUMMARY

Financial management is the process of planning and controlling of the financial resources of a firm. It includes the acquisition, allocation and management of firms' financial resources. It is concerned with how best to manage an organization's resources in order to make sure that the resources are maximized fully.

The major objective of management is to maximize the shareholders' wealth. The shareholders' wealth is the present value of future cash flows or present value of future dividends payable to the shareholders infinitely.

SELF-ASSESSMENT EXERCISE

1. Explain the concept of "Financial Management".
2. State the primary objective of financial management
3. What are the functions of financial manager/roles of financial management?

6.0 TUTOR-MARKED ASSIGNMENTS (TMAS)

1. Define Financial Management. Briefly describe functions of Financial Management.
2. Describe the role of a finance manager.
3. Wealth maximization is the real objective of Financial Management as it helps in financial decisions. Explain this statement.

UNIT 2   SOURCES OF FINANCE

CONTENTS

1.0   INTRODUCTION

In this unit, we will examine the sources of finance available to organizations. There are different forms and sources of finance available to the firm. These are both internal and external; they may be used singularly or in combination. The term "source of business finance" is used to refer to the means by which an entrepreneur raises capital to establish and operate the business of his/her choice.

2.0   OBJECTIVES

At the end of this unit, you should be able to:

*   state the different sources of finance
*   explain some basic concepts such as right issue, preference share and commercial papers.

3.0   MAIN CONTENT

3.1   Short Term Sources of Finance

Short term sources of finance are financing sources up to one-year duration (i.e. they are repayable within one year). It is suitable for funding shortages in working capital. They should not, if it can be avoided, be used to finance a long-term investment. A company that funds long term project with short term funds may be forced to renegotiate a long-term loan under unfavorable condition or to sell the asset, which is needed for the continuation of the business. In addition, where short term sources are recalled by the holders, a company might find itself in a position of technical or legal bankruptcy.

The main methods of obtaining short-term funds are:

i.   Borrowing from friends and relations
ii.   Borrowing from co-operatives
iii.   Trade credits (Suppliers) involves buying of goods on credit. In other words, it is the purchase or sales of goods or equipment whose payment would be effective at a future date. It is a facility granted to a company by a supplier since the system allows the company to pay at a later date. The cost of cash discount is depicted as follows:

Cost of Cash Discount (Implied cost) = $\dfrac{\text{\% Discount}}{100\% - \%\text{Discount}} \times \dfrac{365}{MP - MD}$

Where:

MP = Maximum payment period
MD = Maximum discount period
Definition of terms used in short sources of finance:

a.   **Accruals** - These are deferred payment on items like salaries and wages, rent, tax. Accruals are amount owing on services rendered to firms for which payments have not been made. The amount owed is a source of finance. Example, wages and tax payable.

b.   **Bank borrowing** -This usually takes two forms namely: Bank overdraft (E.g. Drawings against unclear effect facility) and Bank loan facility. Bank overdraft means that the bank allows the company to withdraw more than the amount the company has in its account with bank. The bank charges interest on the amount overdrawn outstanding at any time.
Bank rate is negotiable with Central Bank of Nigeria requirements and the cost to the company is calculated as follows:

Cost of the overdraft = $\dfrac{\text{Interest payment}}{\text{Total sum utilized}} \times \dfrac{365}{\text{Period of Loans}}$

c.   **Factors to consider before granting bank borrowing:**

    i.   The purpose for which the advance is required
    ii.   The Amount of the advance
    iii.   The Repayment term of the advance

iv.   The Term of payment (i.e. how could the advance be paid?)

v.   The Collateral security of the advance

vi.   Does the Character or record of the customer justify the advance?

vii.   What is the Capital structure of the borrowing company?

viii.   How Credible/Credit-worthy are the owners of the business?

d.   Documents to be requested before granting bank borrowing:

i.   Application requesting for the loans.

ii.   Memorandum of Association

iii.   Articles of Association

iv.   Names, Address & Particulars of the Directors

v.   List of directors' shareholdings

vi.   Boards Resolution

vii.   Certificate of Incorporation

viii.   Collateral Security including personal guarantee of the Managing Director.

ix.   Audited Account of the company.

xi.   Management Accounts & Reports of the company.

xii.   Cash flow projection of the company.

xiii.   Acceptance of the offer letter (by affixing company seal & two directors or a director & secretary must sign on behalf of the company).

e.   **Speeding up payment from Trade debtors (Customers)** - This depends on the availability of sound credit control and reminder system.

f.   **Debt Factoring** - A factor is an agent that manages trade debts. Factoring involves turning over the responsibility for collecting a firm's debt to specialist institution. A factor agent usually offers three main services namely:

a.   Taking over the management of client's sales ledger

b.   Insuring their clients against the risk of bad debts.

c.   Providing finance by means of advances against the security of trade debtors

g.   **Bill of Exchange** - This is a form of short term finance used in trade financing. A bill of exchange is one method of settlement in a trade between a seller and a buyer. A bill of exchange takes two forms:

i.   Trade Bills - These are bills of exchange in which the buyer acknowledges it by writing accepted across it and signing it.

ii.   Bank bills - These are bills or exchange drawn on a bank, which will accept them. This is known as acceptance credit.

h.   **Invoice Discounting** - This is similar to factoring except that only the financing service is used meaning that the copies of company's invoices sent to customers are discounted with a financial institution and the trading company still collects the debt as agents for the financial institution and remits the cash on receipt to the account open for that purpose.

i.   **Commercial paper** - This is a short term and an unsecured money market instrument used to invest company's surplus. Large companies with good credit rating can raise short-term funds by issuing commercial notes, which are then purchased by investors in the money market. The financial institution does not guarantee the notes but assists in finding investors to buy them. The investors effectively lend directly to the company issuing the notes. The financial institution charges commission for the service. The commercial papers are issued at discount and have maturities ranging between 2 or 3 days to 270 days. The marketability is weak, there is high tendency for default risk. They, however, attract higher returns than treasury bills.

3.2   Medium Term Sources of Finance

These are financing sources between 1 to 5 years' duration. Some of the medium term sources of finance include:

i.   **Medium Term loans**: These are usually issued for a definite period when compared with overdraft. This is a negotiated loan between a financial institution and a company between 1-5 years, usually at a fixed rate of interest. Medium Term Loans in form of bank lending can be secured or unsecured. Unsecured lending is not common and is only available to credit worthy companies. Secured lending requires heavy collateral securities and proper evaluation of credit worthiness of all customers are also considered.

ii.   **Hire purchase agreement**: This is in form of a credit sales agreement by which the owner of the assets or supplier grant the purchaser the right to take possession of the assets but ownership will not pass until all the hire purchase payment has been paid. The purchaser will pay the hire purchase payment over an agreed period. No form of collateral is required. It is normally reflected in the balance sheet of the borrower. It reduces the gearing ratio and increases ability to raise further finance. It also attracts capital allowance.

iii.   **Lease**: A lease is a contractual agreement between the owner of an asset (lessor) and the user of the asset (lessee) granting the user or lessee the exclusive right to use the asset for an agreed period in return for the payment of rent. The main advantage of lending to a lessee is the use of an asset without having to buy. This conserves an organization's funds. There are two major types of lease:

a.   Finance leases (or full payment leases/ capital leases): The finance lease is non-cancellable. The lessee is responsible for the upkeep, insurance and maintenance of the leased asset. Finance lease is an example of off-balance sheet financing. It is off balance sheet because sources of financing fixed asset are not shown as liabilities on the balance sheet.

b.   Operating leases: With operating lease, the owner (lessor) is responsible for the upkeep, insurance, servicing and maintenance of the leased asset

iv.   **Sales and leaseback**: This is an arrangement by which a firm sells its assets to a financial institution for cash and the financial institution immediately leases it back to the firm.

v.   **Venture capital**: This is a major source of capital for SMEs and collapsed businesses. The provider of finance might decide to participate in the company instead of allowing the client to run the business himself. The participation might be in the form of equity or debenture stock. Small companies normally require this type of finance because of their inadequate collateral securities and poor management skills and talents. It is otherwise known as *business angel*.

vi.   **Project finance**: This requires evaluation of the company and its project. The project itself serves as a collateral security for the fund. It is a risky source of finance if the project fails. However, the financial institution should request for additional collateral security.

3.3   Long Term Sources

These are financing sources of 5 years and more duration. Long term sources of finance include:

i.   **Loan Stock/Debentures**: This is long-term debt finance raised by a company for which interest is paid usually at a fixed rate. The company must pay the interest whether it makes profit or not. Loan stock also has a nominal value of 100. Debentures are a form of loan stock that is legally defined as the written acknowledgement of a debt incurred by a company usually given under company seal and containing provisions as to the payment of interest and eventual repayment of principal.

Loan stock and debentures are often secured. The security can take the form of *fixed charge* (usually on a specific asset/ property). *Floating charges* (charge on certain asset of the company e.g. stock/property). Floating charges can crystallize to a specific security if the company defaults in meeting its obligations under the terms of loan/debenture. Loan stock/debentures also are unsecured.

However only high credit-worthy companies can issue unsecured loan stock. The interest on unsecured loan stock is usually higher than that of a secured loan stock. Loan stock and debentures are usually redeemable, irredeemable and convertible. The interest payments on loan stock/debentures are allowable for corporation tax.

The higher the loan stock/debentures in a company's capital structure, the higher the gearing or leverage. Gearing or leverage increases financial risk of a company since interest must be paid irrespective of profitability.

ii. **Preference Shares**: The holders of preference shares are entitled to a fixed percentage dividend before ordinary shareholders can be paid any dividend. Preference shares are a form of hybrid security between ordinary shares and debentures. These are often issued as an alternative to debt when the company pays no tax. Preference shares can be redeemable or irredeemable.

iii. **Ordinary Shares**: Ordinary shareholders are the owners of the firm. They exercise control over the firm through their voting rights. A firm contemplating on raising funds through ordinary shares will incur floatation cost/issue cost.

Ways of Raising Ordinary Shares

iv   **Public Subscription (Stock Exchange Introduction)**: This is an invitation to the public at large so as to invite them to subscribe for share in the company. The public issue must comply with CAMA 1990. This is also known as Initial Public Offering (IPO).

Techniques of Conversion

a.   **Conversion Price (CP)**: It is the nominal value of convertible security that can be converted into one ordinary share. It represents the effective price of ordinary shares paid for on conversion. CP can be derived as follows:

Conversion Price = Market Value/Nominal value of Convertible security

Number of ordinary shares issued on conversion

b. **Conversion Rate (CR)**: It is the number of convertible security that could be exchanged for new ordinary shares or security. It is expressed as follows:

Conversion Rate= Number of ordinary shares issued on conversion
Market value/nominal value of converted security

c. **Conversion Value (CV):** It is the market value of ordinary shares into which unit of stock or convertible security will be converted. This is expressed as follows:

Conversion Value = Conversion Rate **X** Market Value per share

d. **Cost of option to convert**: At the point of conversion, the holder of such security has two options i.e. to convert and not to convert. The cost of option is derived as follows:

Cost of option = Actual price of convertible security Conversion price
Conversion Rate

e. **Conversion Premium/Discount**: This is the difference between the conversion price and market price.

It should be noted that:

i) Where conversion price is greater than (>) market price of share, it is equal to discount.

ii) Conversion premium/discount could be presented in form of yield i.e.

Conversion Yield is known as: Premium/Discount X
Conversion Price   1

1. **Bonus/Script/Capitalization issue**: This is issued to existing shareholders by whom further shares are credited as fully paid-up out of the company's reserves in proportion to existing holdings. This is known as capitalization of reserves.

2. **Offer for sale**: This is where a company issues its shares for public subscription through an issuing house in which the sales proceeds go to the existing shareholders not the company. Simply put, offer for sale is the sale of existing shares by existing shareholders but not a fresh issue of shares. This method was used by Daar Communication Plc. and all the proceeds were paid directly into Daar Holding Plc. for the existing shareholders of the company.

3. **Offer for Sale by Tender**: This is when a company's share is being issued out by a company to the public asking the price that all intending shareholders can subscribe. This is referred to as striking

price and the stock exchange will ensure that all shares are taken up at the striking price.

4. **Retained Earnings**: This is a part of a company's profit not paid out as ordinary dividend. It is also a source of financing. It is a cheap source of raising finance as compared to share issue because no issue cost is involved. Raising funds through retained earnings avoid dilution of control since there is no share issue to outside N Retained earnings are an important source of financing for companies that do not have access to the capital markets.

The table below is a summary of the sources of finance.

Table 1.0: Summary of Sources of Finance

SHORT TERM SOURCES	MEDIUM TERM SOURCES	LONG TERM SOURCES
• Bank credit	• Term loan	• Equity
• Commercial papers	• Venture capital	• Initial Public Offer (IPO)
• Trade credits	• Project finance	• Seasoned Offer
• Factoring	• Sale and Leaseback	• Hot issue
• Invoice discounting	• Hire Purchase	• Gun jumping
• Bills discounting	• Mortgage	• Debentures
• Accruals		• Preference share capital
• Bankers acceptance		
• Franchising		

4.0   SUMMARY

In this unit, we examined the three major sources of finance and the prerequisites for each source.

5.0   CONCLUSION

The business organization must ensure that their business is finance using the cheapest and the most convenient sources for the highest effectiveness. It is therefore of value to consider the various sources of finance to the business organization

SELF-ASSESSMENT EXERCISE

Briefly explain the three major sources of finance

6.0   TUTOR-MARKED ASSIGNMENT

1.   Explain the various ways of sourcing for finance.
2.   Explain each of the following:
      (a) Preference share
      (b) Ordinary share
      (c) Venture capital
      (d) Lease
3.   State five (5) factors to be considered before granting bank borrowing.
4.   Mention at least five (5) documented requested before granting bank borrowing.

UNIT 3   COST OF CAPITAL

CONTENTS

1.0   INTRODUCTION

Cost of capital is an integral part of investment decision as it is used to measure the worth of investment proposal provided by the business concern. It is used as a discount rate in determining the present value of future cash flows associated with capital projects. Cost of capital is also called as cut-off rate, target rate, hurdle rate and required rate of return.

When the firms are using different sources of finance, the finance manager must take careful decision with regard to the cost of capital; because it is closely associated with the value of the firm and the earning capacity of the firm.

In this unit, we shall examine cost of capital, its usage and various types.

2.0   OBJECTIVES

At the end of this unit, you should be able to:

●   Understand the meaning of cost of capital and its usefulness
●   Examine the opportunity Cost of Capital

3.0   MAIN CONTENT

3.1   Cost of Capital

Cost of capital is the rate of return that a firm must earn on its project investments to maintain its market value and attract funds. Cost of capital is the required rate of return on its investments which belongs to equity, debt and retained earnings. If a firm fails to earn return at the expected rate, the market value of the shares will fall and it will result in the reduction of overall wealth of the shareholders.

In other words, cost of capital is the minimum required rate of return on investment. It is the present value of future stream of Net Cash flow on investment. It is also the minimum value per share in the capital market.

3.2   The Usefulness of Cost of Capital

i.   It is an important tool in capital budgeting decision.
ii.   It is a useful measurement of the firm's financial performance
iii.   It is a tool of financial decision making.
iv.   It can be used in selecting source of finance; as cost of capital the market is known the Financial Manager can select a cheap source of fund.
v.   It is also important in dividend policy formulation and working capital management.

3.3   Types of Cost

i.   **Future Cost***:* Are expected cost associated with investment.
       They are those costs used in appraising investment opportunities when matched with future benefits or expected returns on the investment, it will produce the net return on such investment. Future cost of fund is also used as discounting factor.
ii.   **Historical Cost***:* These are past financial expenditures used in securing a future benefit. It is the sacrificing of present consumption (in investment) for future consumption benefit.
iii.   *Explicit Cost:* The explicit cost of capital is that cost of capital that equates the present value of future incremental cash inflow with present value of future incremental cash outflow. That is, the cost of debt, equity etc.
iv.   **Opportunity Cost of Capital/Explicit Cost of Capital:** It is the cost of alternative project forgone for the purpose of investing in the selected projects. Explicit cost of capital becomes relevant only

when there are several possible investment opportunities to be selected from.

3.4 Valuation of Securities
Debt (Irredeemable debenture)

The cost of Debt is the internal rate of return on Debt; that is the cost at which the present value of incremental cash inflow equals the present market value (or purchase cost) of the asset.

$$N_0 = 1(1 + r)^{-1} + (1 + r)^{-2} + I(1 + r)^{-3} + EI_n(1 + r)^{-n}$$

$I = 1$ or $1 = I$

Where
N_0 = Net cash inflow in year zero
I_n = Cash inflow in year 1 to year n
N = Number of years
R = Interest rate

Note: This is the cost of irredeemable Debt. For example, debenture.

Illustration I
Kim purchased a 15% irredeemable debenture for $100 ex-interest.Compute the cost of debt.

Solution

Cost of Debt = $\dfrac{15 \times 100}{100}$ = $15

Cost of Redeemable Deb (Debenture)
The cost of redeemable debt is calculated using the internal rate of return method. This represents the discount rate that equates the current market value (ex-interest) of the debenture with the present value of associated future cash inflows. These are the interest payable annually plus the redemption value in the year of redemption:

$$V_{RD} = \frac{I}{(1 + r)^1} + \frac{I}{(1 + r)^2} + \frac{I}{(1 + r)^3} + \dots + \frac{R}{(1 + r)^n}$$

Where
$R(1 + r)^{-1}$ = Present value of redemption value
V_{RD} = Value of redeemable debenture
R = Interest rate
I = Interest recovered

Illustration 2

Cole bought a 12% redeemable debenture, redeemable at par in 10 years' time. The current market value of the debenture is $80, associated tax is 40%. What is the cost of the redeemable debenture?

Solution

Yr 0   Current market value   = $80 (outflow)
Yr 1 - 10 Interest net of tax   = $12 (1- 0.4)   = $7.20
Yr.10 Redemption value= $100 at par inflow

Time	NCF	NCF 10%	PV	DCF at 13%	PV
Yr 0	80	1	(80)	1	(80)
Yr 1-10	7.20	6.144	44.24	5.426	39.067
Yr 10	100	0.38	38.00	0.29	29
			2.24		(11.933)

By interpolation,
IRR =

$$10 + \frac{2.24}{(2.24 + 11.931)} (13 - 10) \left.\right\} = \underline{10\%} \left\{\right.$$

3.5   Cost of Preference Share

Irredeemable preference share/redeemable preference share
Preference share is assumed to be debt in nature because a preference shareholder is entitled to fix Dividend like the Debenture holder that earns fix interest rate. Thus in computing the cost of preference shareholder same method used in Debenture cost calculation is used.
Cost of irredeemable preference share will be.
Cost of irredeemable preference share:

$No = D (1 + Kp)^{-1} + D (1 + kp)^{-2} + D (1 + kp)^{-3}$
Where No = Net cash inflow in year zero
Kp = Rate of return on preference share
D = Dividend received
           R = Number of year.
Redeemable preference share
$$V_{RP} = \frac{I}{(1 + kp)^1} + \frac{I}{(1 + kp)^2} + \frac{I}{(1 + kp)^3} + \frac{I}{(1 + kp)^n}$$

Note: This can only be solved by using interpolation i.e. the internal rate of return method.

Cost of Equity (Ordinary Share)

The ordinary share is irredeemable, they earn dividend however the dividend can be growing dividend; that is, where the Dividend grows at a particular rate annually.

$$K_E = \frac{D}{P}$$

Where K_E = Cost of equity
D = Dividend
P = Market value
G = Growth rate.

Cost of Equity with Issuing or Floatation Cost

$$K_E = \frac{D \quad P}{- X}$$

Where D = Dividend
K_E = Cost of equity
X = Flotation or issuing cost.

Illustration 3

The issue price of a share is ₦30 and issue cost are 30k per share. New shareholders expect constant annual dividend of 50 kobo. What is the cost of equity?

$$KE = \frac{0.5}{30 - 0.3} = \frac{0.50}{29.7} = 0.0168 = \underline{1.682\%}$$

Dividend Growth Model

No shareholder in real life expect a constant dividend for a long time his investment. Thus most times the dividend is assumed to increase or grow annually.

$$MV\ (Ex\text{-}div) = \frac{D_0(I+g) + D(I+g)^2 + D(1+g)_n}{(I + ke \quad (I+ke)^2 \quad (I+ke)^n}$$

Most time a constant dividend increase for perpetuity is assumed.

$$MV = \frac{D_0(I+g)}{Ke-g}$$

$$KE = \frac{D(I+g) + g}{MV}$$

$$KE = \frac{d}{MV} + g$$

Where

$$D \quad = D(1+g) = \text{Dividend in year 1}$$
$$KE \quad = \text{Cost of share}$$
$$MV \quad = \text{Market value.}$$

Growth Calculation:

$$g = \sqrt[(n-1)]{\dfrac{\text{Latest Dividend}}{\text{Earliest Dividend}}}$$

Gordon Model of Dividend Growth Calculation

$$g \quad = rb$$
$$b \quad = \text{retention rate}$$
$$r \quad = \text{return on capital employed rate}$$

i.e. return rate on capital employed

$$\dfrac{EPS}{APS} \quad = \quad \dfrac{\text{Earning per share}}{\text{Asset per share}}$$

$$\dfrac{b}{EPS} \quad = \quad \dfrac{EPS - DPS}{}$$

$$\dfrac{rb}{(EPS \quad APS)} \quad = \quad \dfrac{(EPS - DPS \; X \; EPS)}{APS} \quad = \quad \dfrac{EPS - DPS}{}$$

4.0   SUMMARY

The method of calculating the various cost of financial assets was discussed which include ordinary share debenture and other bond. The various techniques of those appraisals and their market value was also discussed in this unit.

4.1   CONCLUSION

The student will be able to apply the knowledge gained in making market decision on when to use means of finance and when not to use them. It will be of value in deciding whether to go for finance by equity or debt.

SELF-ASSESSMENT EXERCISE

Explain the major usefulness of cost of capital

6.0   TUTOR-MARKED ASSIGNMENT

1.   Explain the meaning and various types of cost.
2.   Identify the Importance of Cost of Preference Share.

MODULE 2

UNIT 1   CAPITAL BUDGETING UNDER UNCERTAINTY 1

CONTENTS

1.0   INTRODUCTION

The financial manager in any organization must decide which investment opportunity must be accepted among available ones. The risk and return factor on such investments must be given adequate thought. To successfully accomplish these, the financial manager will have to appraise available investment opportunities to ensure making the right decision.

In view of the foregoing, we therefore examine, in this unit and subsequent unit capital budgeting as well as the methods of appraising it.

2.0   OBJECTIVES

At the end of this unit, you should be able to:

*   define capital budgeting
*   state the need and importance of capital budgeting
*   mention the procedures involved in capital budgeting
*   state the characteristics of capital budgeting

• discuss the methods of evaluating capital budgeting.

3.0   MAIN CONTENT

3.1   Definition of Capital Budgeting

Capital budgeting decision can be defined as the firm's decision to invest its current funds in most efficient long term projects. It is the commitment of organization's current funds in a long term project with the aim of profit making. It is a common practice in modern businesses for funds to be committed on the acquisition of land, building, machinery and other capital project with a view to earning in the future an income, which is greater than the funds committed. In other words, capital budgeting is the process whereby decisions are taken on how capital funds shall deployed. It includes the appraisal of proposed investment projects by reference to their expected returns and to the cost of capital (Yusuf & Bolarinwa, 2010; Ogunniyi, 2010).

3.2 Need and Importance of Capital Budgeting

i.   **Huge investments:** Capital budgeting requires huge investments of funds, but the available funds are limited, therefore the firm before investing projects, plan are control its capital expenditure.

ii.   **Long-term:** Capital expenditure is long-term in nature or permanent in nature.
       Therefore, financial risks involved in the investment decision are more. If higher risks are involved, it needs careful planning of capital budgeting.

iii.   **Irreversible:** The capital investment decisions are irreversible, are not changed back. Once the decision is taken for purchasing a permanent asset, it is very difficult to dispose off those assets without involving huge losses.

iv.   **Long-term effect:** Capital budgeting not only reduces the cost but also increases the revenue in long-term and will bring significant changes in the profit of the company by avoiding over or more investment or under investment. Over investments leads to be unable to utilize assets or over utilization of fixed assets.

Therefore, before making the investment, it is required carefully planning and analysis of the project thoroughly.

3.3   Kinds of Capital Budgeting Decisions

The overall objective of capital budgeting is to maximize the profitability. If a firm concentrates return on investment, this objective can be achieved either by increasing the revenues or reducing the costs. The increasing revenues can be achieved by expansion or the size of operations by adding a new product line. Reducing costs mean representing obsolete return on assets.

3.4   Procedures Involved in Capital Budgeting Decisions

The procedures involved in capital budgeting decisions are as follows:

i.   Identification of possible projects
ii.   Evaluation of projects
iii.   Authorization of projects
iv.   Development
v.   Monitoring and control of projects
vi.   Post audit

3.5   Characteristics of Capital Budgeting

Capital expenditures differ from day-to-day 'revenue' expenditure because:

i.   They involve large outlay.
ii.   The benefits will accrue over a long period of time, usually well over one year and often much longer, so that the benefits cannot all be set against costs in the current year's profit and loss account.
iii   They are very risky.
iv.   They involve irreversible decision.

3.6   Methods of Capital Budgeting Evaluation

By matching the available resources and projects it can be invested. The funds available are always living funds. There are many considerations taken for investment decision process such as environment and economic conditions.

The methods of evaluations are classified as follows:

(A)   Traditional methods (or Non-discount methods)
     (i)   Pay-back Period Methods

(ii)   Accounting Rate of Return

(B)   **Modern methods (or Discount methods)**

    (i)   Net Present Value Method

    (ii)   Internal Rate of Return Method

    (iii)   Profitability Index Method

In this unit, we shall discuss only the traditional methods.

These are explained in seriatim.

3.6 The Payback Period Method

The principle behind the Pay back method has more regard for liquidity than profitability. It is a measure of liquidity over cost (or initial outlay).

Advantages of Pay Back Period

1.   It is easy to understand and estimate.
2.   It is liquidity based; rather than profitability, thus seems more acceptable where liquidity stands as the main factor to be considered.
3.   It is less forecast biased sensitive, unlike other investment criterion used.
4.   It is suitable for use in an unstable economic environment

Disadvantages of Pay Back Period

1.   It disregards the time value of money.
2.   It disregards all cash inflows which occur after the payback period.
3.   It is not an objective criterion for decision-making
4.   If it is not properly applied (Invoked). It may lead to wrong decision-making
5.   It is highly subjective in nature.

Illustration 1

Two projects A and B with the following relevant information

Project A: Outlay = 200,000

Inflows year 1 = 60,000 Year2 = 80,000, Year 3 = 80,000 Year 4 =100,000.

Project B: Outlay = 200,000

Inflows Year 1 = 80,000 Year 2 = 80,000 Year 3 = 40,000 Year 4 = 60,000

Year 5 = 60,000

Required: Compute the payback period.
SOLUTION

Project A	Cash flow	Cumulative
Y0	**(200,000)**	**(200,000)**
Y1	60,000	140,000
Y2	80,000	60,000
Y3	80,000	
Y4	100,000	

Actual payback = 2 Years + $\frac{60,000}{80,000}$ Years

2 yrs + 0.75 yrs = 2.75 years

Project B	Cash flow	Cumulative
Y0	**(200,000)**	**(200,000)**
Y1	80,000	120,000
Y2	80,000	40,000
Y3	40,000	
Y4	60,000	
Y4	60,000	

N.B: Where there is equal annual cash inflow or where the stream of cash inflow is the same over the life span of the project, then the pay back formula becomes.

$$pbp= \frac{I}{Cn}$$

Where:
I =   Initial cash outlay
   Annual cash inflow

In the above fisher's interception model, Project A intercept pro at remaking project B more preferable.

N.B In the above illustration, the payback period of project A is cumbersome to ascertain from the tabulated computation. This is largely due to the fact that the streams of cash inflows are the same over period of the project's life. Thus, a formula will help to allay this uncertainty, in the case where the streams of cash inflows are not the same over the life span of project.

Payback period $= L + \dfrac{I - CFL}{A(L+1)}$

Where

L = the last complete year in which cumulative net cash are less than the initial investment (outlay)

I = initial cash outlay (investment)

CFL = Cumulative cash inflow at period L

A (L+I) Actual cash inflows at the period immediately after period by applying the above formula, we have to identity the last period with negative cumulative flows i.e.-(60,000) for Yr2: -It -is discovered that at the end of this Yr2 (2nd year) $140,000 out of the $200;000 has been realized. Meaning that the remaining $60,000 difference has to be accounted for in the 3rd year say mid of the Yr3.

3.7 Accounting Rate of Return

The Accounting Rate of Return (ARR) is otherwise known as the Average Return on Investment. It is used in measuring the rate of return to investment.

The formula used is as follows:

ARR = $\dfrac{\text{Average profit}}{\text{Average investment}}$

Where:

Average profit (AP) = $\dfrac{\text{Total Profit Generated}}{\text{No of years}}$

Average investment = $\dfrac{\text{Initial cash outlay}}{2}$

3.7.1 Advantages of Accounting Rate of Return

1. It is simple to calculate
2. It uses readily available accounting data.
3. It considers the profits over the entire life of the project.
4. It could be used to compare performance of many companies.

3.7.2 Disadvantages of Accounting Rate of Return

1. It ignores risk and management's attitude to risk.
2. It takes no cognizance of the time value of money.
3. It can be calculated in several ways.

4. It uses accounting profit rather than cash as the measure of benefit.

Illustration 2

Adams & Co. invested $300,000 in a certain investment yielding the following cash inflow after tax:

Year 1:   100,000
Year 2:   200,000
Year 3:   50,000
Year 4:   40,000

Given that the life span of the investment is 4 years.
compute the average Return on Investment ROI or ARR

SOLUTION

$$\text{Average profit} = \frac{100,000 + 200,000 + 50,000 + 40,000}{4}$$

$$` = \frac{390,000}{4}$$

$$= 97,500$$

$$\text{Average investment} = \frac{300,000}{2} = 150,000$$

$$\text{ROI or ARR} = \frac{97,500}{150,000} = 0.65$$

$$\text{ROI or ARR} = 65\%$$

4.0   SUMMARY

The various methods of appraising investment project, particularly the traditional method, were covered in this unit. This is meant to be a guide to manager in decision making which involves capital project.

5.0   CONCLUSION

In making decision, as to the kinds of project to be embarked upon, the payback period, the accounting rate of return among others can be used to determine the viability and profitability of investment project and be able to identify those the firm can engage in and those they will not accept based on their profitability or otherwise.

SELF-ASSESSMENT EXERCISE

1. What is capital budgeting?
2. Mention any three needs for capital budgeting.
3. What are the procedures involved in capital budgeting decisions?

4.   State any 5 characteristics of capital budgeting.

6.0   TUTOR-MARKED ASSIGNMENTS (TMAS)

1.   Explain the merits and demerits of payback period
2.   Identify the major features of Investment Appraisal Method
3.   State the merits and demerits of accounting rate of return

UNIT 2   CAPITAL BUDGETING UNDER UNCERTAINTY 2

CONTENTS

1.0   INTRODUCTION

As discussed in unit 1 of this module, there are two major groups of investment appraisal methods. The first group being the traditional method which considers the time value of money; while the second group that is the modern method does not give any cognizance to the time value of money.

In this unit, we shall discuss the second group – the modern/discounted cash flow method.

2.0   OBJECTIVES

At the end of this unit, you should be able to:

•   explain the investment appraisal method under discount methods
•   identify the problems associated with Net Present Value Method, Internal Rate of Return, Profitability Index,

3.0   MAIN CONTENT

3.1   The Modern/Discounted Cash Flow Method of Investment Appraisal

The modern/discounted cash flow method of investment appraisal, unlike the traditional method, does not give cognizance to the time value of money. This method is superior to the ARR and PBP techniques earlier discussed.

The methods include:

(i)   Net Present Value Method
(ii)   Internal Rate of Return Method
(iii)   Profitability Index Method

These methods are discussed below, and the following points should be noted:

i.   Time Value of Money
The net present value and the Internal Rate of Return (IRR) incorporate time value of money. The time value of money concept states that the value of $1 today will not be the same in a year's time, due to depreciation in the real value of dollar. In order words, what a dollar can buy today in a year's time an amount above a dollar would be required to purchase that same article. Thus a dollar invested today should yield an amount over and above the dollar invested. Devaluation of money allows for this. However, in a relatively stable economy, the interest rate could be taking to account for devaluation in dollar. The interest rate per dollar is the compensation for the loss of value by the naira amount. Hence the interest rate is used for discounting.

ii.   Money and Real Interest Rate
The scientific method assumes therefore that the interest rate used is the real interest rate and not the money interest rate. The real interest rate is the after tax interest rate while the money interest rate is the before tax interest rate. The scientific method makes use of the real interest rate asking for granted that inflation rate will be equal the tax rate. Since normally the value of good should only be inflated by the tax paid thereon.

For example, the money interest rate is 20% and the tax rate is 30% the real interest rate will be (1-0.30) (20%) = (0.70) (20%) = 14%.

3.1.1   Net Present Value Method

The net present value method is the total present value of a project which should be greater than the initial capital outlay of the project before such project could be accepted. The decision rule is that:

i.   When total present value > capital outlay: **Accept the project with positive NPV**

ii.   When total present value < capital outlay: **Reject the project with negative NPV**

Illustration 1

A company wishes to invest $400,000 in a project which has a 6-year life span. With Net cash inflow is as follows:

Year 1   100,000

Year 2   20,000

Year 3   50,000

Year 4   60,000

Year 5   100,000

Year 6   100,000.

The cost of capital is 10%. Should this project be accepted?

SOLUTION

Time	Cash Flow	DCF (10%)	FV
Year 0	400,000	1.000	(400,000)
Year 1	100,000	0.909	90900
Year 2	200,000	0.826	165200
Year 3	50,000	0.75 1	37550
Year 4	60,000	0.683	40980
Year 5	100,000	0.621	62100
Year 6	100, 000	0.564	56400
		NPV	**53130**

Decision Rule

Since the present value is more than the initial outlay we will accept the project.

3.1.2 Internal Rate Return

The internal rate of return (IRR) is the interest rate which produces a cumulative present value that is equal to the initial outlay.

$$P_0 = \sum_{n-1}^{T} \frac{P}{(1+r)^t}$$

$$\sum_{n-1}^{t} R_n(1+r)^{-n} \qquad \sum_{n-1}^{t} C_n (1+r)^{-n}$$

Where r = internal rate of return. The internal rate of return method helps to strike the point where the present value of inflows equals the initial outlay. That is NPV= Cumulative present Value-Initial outlay =0

Linear Interpolation

Using the principle of similar triangle, a formula could be obtained for the internal rate of return. This method entails deriving two Net Present Values (NPVs) from two interest rates applied. One of the two NPVs must be negative and the other positive. These Net present values and the associated interest rates can now be used to secure the internal rate of return. It is otherwise known as Linear Interpolation Method: This is the short cut method of getting the correct internal rate of return. When you tried at discount rate A, and the NPV is positive, try another rate B that gives you a negative NPV. When you get a negative NPV, then stop and interpolate using the formulae below:

IRR $= A + \dfrac{a}{a+b} (B-A)$

Where

A =is one discount Interest rate.

B =the other discount rate

a = is the NPV at rate A.

b= is the NPV at rate B

ILLUSTRATION 2

A company wishes to invest a sum of $350,000 in a project view the following net cash inflows for 5 years

Year 1   200,000

Year 2   100,000

Year 3   100,000

Year 4   40,000

Year 5   10,000

The acceptable interest rate is 10%.
You are required to compute

1)   The Net present value
2)   Internal rate of return for the project

SOLUTION

Time	Cash Flow	DCF (10%)	PV	DCF (16%)	PV
Year 0	(350,000)	1	(350,000)	1	(350,000)
Year 1	200,000	0.909	181800	0.862	172400
Year 2	100,000	0.826	82600	0.743	74300
Year 3	100,000	0.751	75100	0.641	64100
Year 4	40,000	0.683	27320	0.552	22080
Year 5	10,000	0.620	6200	0.476	4760
			23020		**(12360)**

2.   To compute IRR$= A + \dfrac{a(B- A)}{(a + b)}$

$10\% + \dfrac{23020}{[23020 + 12360]}$ (16-10)

$10\% + 3.90 = 13.90$

OR

$16 - \dfrac{12360}{[23020 + 12360]}$ (16-10)

16-2.096

= 13.90

PROBLEM WITH NPV

There are several problems inhibiting the usage of NPV as a method of project evaluation.

1.   **Multiple Internal Rates of Return:**
        This is a situation whereby a negative inflow occurs during the
        project's life. While the Net present value of the project is still

positive in this case multiple internal rates of return will exist thus making our result ambiguous.

2. **The Re-investment Rate Problem of the IRR and NPV**
The internal rate of return assumes that cash inflows are re-invested at the internal rate of return margin.

On the other hand the Net present value (NPV) principle assumes that inflows of cash are reinvested at the NPV rate. This can yield a different final result.

Two projects with the same internal rate of return of 20%

Project	Price	Cash inflow (yr$_1$)	Cash inflow (yr$_2$)
A	75	15	19
B	75	60	36

The company reinvested at a rate of 3% per annum.

Project 1
Yr 1   15 x 1.03 = 15.45
Yr 2 inflow   = 19.00
                       34.45

Project 2
Yr 1   60 x 1.03   = 61.8
Yr 2 inflow   = 36.0
                      97.8

3. **Independency of Project (3):** The Net present value principle (NPV) assumes that project A is different from project B, project B is different from project C etc.

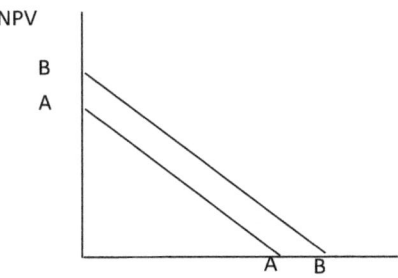

In the above, project B must always be preferred to A. However, this may not always hold. In a situation of Non-independence where a project is assumed to be the best now turns out to be false off.

Advantages of NPV
1. It considers the time value of money unlike the payback period
2. It considers the cash inflows both during and after the period i.e. over the project's entire life.

Disadvantages of NPV
1. It is cumbersome and difficult to compute.
2. It is not suitable for project with different cash inflows

Net Terminal Value (NTV)
The net terminal value is a compounded value of the net present value of the life of an asset or project obtained by compounding all the cash flows to the end year of the life span of the project.

Illustration 4
A project cost N250 with cash inflow of

Year 1   60
Year 2   120
Year 3   80
Year 4   80

The cost of capital is 10%. Compute the net terminal value of the project.

SOLUTION
There are two methods in solving the above problem.
Method I:

$-250 (1.1)^4 + 60 (1.1)^3 + 120 (1.1)^2 + 80(1.1)' + 80(1.1)°$
$-250 (1.4641) + 60 (1.331) + 120 (1.21) + 80 (1.1) 80 (1)$
$-366.025 + 79.86 + 145.2 + 88 + 80$
$= 27.035$
$= 27.$

Methods 2:
Using the NPV method:

Time	Cash flow	Df (10%)	PV
Year 0	(250)	1	(250)
Year 1	60	0.909	54.54
Year 2	120	0.826	99.12

Year 3	80	0.751	60.08
Year 4	80	0.683	54.64
			18.38

NTV = 18.38 $(1.1)^4$ = 26.91
= 27

3.1.3 Profitability Index or the Benefit Cost Ratio

This is the ratio of present value of project life to the initial capital outlay.

Profitability Index (P.I)   = $\dfrac{PV}{Outlay}$

Or

Profitability Index   = $\dfrac{NPV}{Outlay}$

Illustration 5
From Illustration 4, compute the profitability index of the project.

P.I = $\dfrac{268.38}{250}$

= 1.07352

Illustration 6
ABC Ltd is planning to replace two of his machine with a new model because of the maintenance cost of $5,000. One of the two old machines is considered to be expensive. The old machines are being depreciated over a period of 10 years on a straight line basis. The estimated scrap value after 10 years is $900.00 for each machine while the current market value is estimated at $1,500.00 each. The annual operating costs for each of the old machine are as follows:

	$
Materials	90,000
Barbar- 1 operator for 2,000 hrs	2,025
Variable expenses	1,387
Maintenance (excluding compulsory expenditure	3,000
Fixed expenses: Depreciation	135
Fixed Factory overhead	4,050

The new machine has an estimated life of 8 years and will cost $100,000 made up of ex-showroom price of $87,000.00 and installation cost of 13,000.00. The scrap value after 8 years is estimated at $4,500.00 the operating costs of the new machine are estimated as follows:

	$	$
Materials		162,000
Labour - 3 operators at 1,800 Hrs		3,900
Variable expenses		2,274
Fixed expenses:		

Depreciation	11,938	
Fixed Factory overhead	7,800	
Maintenance	4,500	
	24,238	

The company's cost of capital is 10% and projects are evaluated on basis of rate of returns. In addition to satisfying the profitability test, projects are also required to satisfy a financial viability test by meeting 5 year pay-back condition.

You are required to:

a. Advise management on the profitability of the proposal by applying a discounted cash flow technique to calculate the internal rate of return.

b. Subject proposal to a financial viability test, and

c. Comment very briefly on two other factors that could influence the decision of management in respect of this proposal.

d. (Assume that residual value is received on the last day of the machine's working life and ignore taxation).

Present value of $1 for 8 years

	Annuity
Ordinary	
At 10%	5.335
0.4665	
At 20%	3.837
0.2326	

ANSWER

a.   Operating   Cost   –Old
Machines

	$
Materials $ (90,000 x 2)	180,000
Labour, $ (2025 x 2)	4,050
Variable expenses N(1387 x 2)	2,774
Maintenance	6,000
Total	**192,824**

38

Operating Cost-Proposed Machine

Material	162,000
Labour	3,900
Variable expenses	2,271
Maintenance	4,500
Total	**172,674**

Savings per annum if new machine is bought
= $(192,824 - 172,674)
= $20,150

Internal Rate of Return

NPV AT 10%

Initial Outlay	= $(100,000 – 3,000)	97,000.00
NPV of savings = 20150 x 5.333		107,500.25
NPV of scrap value = 4500 x 0.46645		2,099.25
NPV		12,599.50

NPV at 20%

Initial Outlay (100,000 - 3000)		(97,000)
NPV of savings = 20,150 x 3.837		77,316
NPV of scrap value = 4t,500 x 0.2326		1,046.70
NPV		(18,637,75)

IRR = 10% + [12599.5   ] 20% - 10%
         12599.5 + 18637.75
= 10% + 4%
      = 14%

Financial Viability Test

Yr.	Cash Flow	Cumulative Cash flow
0	-97,000	97,000
1	20,150	76,850
2	20,150	56,700
3	20,150	36,550
4	20,150	16,400
5	20,150	3,750
6	20,150	+23,900
7	20,150	+44,050
8	20,150	+64,200
9	4,500	+63,700

Payback period= 4 year + 16400 x 12 months)
20150
= 4 years + 9.767 months

= 4 years, 10 months.

Two other factors that can influence the decision of management in respect of this proposal are:

(i) **Taxation:** The timing of taxation should especially take capital allowance into consideration. In this type of investment appraisal as this will affect the cash flows from the project.

(ii) **Inflation:** In an inflationary situation, the existing techniques for investment appraisal (NPV, IRR) are inadequate unless certain. Adjustments are made, because real purchasing power is constantly being eroded. Unless this erosion is taken into account company will find that 'profitable' investment could actually turn out to be seriously unprofitable.

4.0   SUMMARY

This unit discussed the major methods of investment appraisal under uncertainty using NPV, IRR and PI methods. Also, the merits and demerits of these methods were presented.

5.0   CONCLUSION

The students can use the internal rate of return, the net present value and the probability index to make decision about the profitability of investment project and be able to identify those the firm can engage in and those they will not accept based on their profitability or otherwise.

SELF-ASSESSMENT EXERCISE

Discuss the problems associated with Net Present Value Method

6.0   TUTOR-MARKED ASSIGNMENTS (TMAs)

1. Explain in detail what you understand by Net Present Value
2. What are the advantages and disadvantages of NPV?
3. What problems are associated with NPV?
4. What is IRR and PI? Explain briefly.

UNIT 3   **WORKING CAPITAL MANAGEMENT**

CONTENTS

1.0   INTRODUCTION

Working capital is the life blood of an organization, it consists the liquidity flow as different from the profitability of the organization. A profitable but illiquid business could be forced to close down. It should be borne in mind that, no matter the amount spent on equipment, plant and machinery, buildings etc., if the ingredients required for production are not efficiently managed, the entire amount committed to the project will become a waste.

This unit therefore examines working capital management.

2.0   OBJECTIVES

At the end of this unit, you should be able to:

•   explain working capital management
•   analyse factors affecting working capital
•   describe the major concepts of working capital
•   identify the operating cycle.

3.0   MAIN CONTENT

3.1   Working Capital

The working capital is the required fund necessary for the day to day running of the business. It is the life blood of an organization. It includes Cash, Inventory, Accounts receivable, Prepayment, (which constitute application of fund) accounts payable, accruals, etc. (which constitute sources of term fund).

The working capital constitutes the short term investment decision of the organization. It is the short term sources and application of fund the cost of these short term sources of fund are very important to an organization. It is the current assets circulating or floating capital. It changes form in the production and trading process. E.g. Cash is used to purchase raw materials (Inventory). These are being used up in the production process to yield finished goods (stock). The stocks are sold for cash or on credit (yielding) account receivables; sometimes inventories (raw material) are obtained on credit (Account payable).

3.1.1 Working Capital Concepts

a.   **The Gross concept:** It is the totality of the current assets of the business which include accounts receivable, cash, short dated securities (short term investment), bill receivable and Stock (or inventory). The gross concept advocates that a firm should possess working capital just adequate and sufficient to meet the firm's operating cycle. It ensures that excess investment in cash is avoided, since excess investment in cash results in excess liquidity resulting to high cost of income. Thus, it is called optimal level of Investment in current assets; excess investment in current asset is avoided.

Secondly, this emphasizes available source of fund‐ such that such fun are called up as at when needed. Excess investment in current asset is thus avoided.

b.   **The Net Concept:** This emphasizes continuous liquidity of the firm. The concept advocates a finance of Working Capital by a permanent source of funds e.g. shares, debentures, long term debts, preference shares, retained earning etc. The Net concept advocates the efficient mix of long term and short term sources of funding working capital.

42

There exists no rule as to the exact Working Capital level a firm should hold and there exists no rule as to how current asset should be financed.

3.2 Factors Affecting Working Capital

i.   The fluctuations necessitated by seasonal sales, change in taste and fashion.

ii. The operating cycle affect the working capital, a long term operating cycle would result into capital tie down and hence increased cost of working capital.

iii. The nature of the business also determines the level and extent of working capital the business will have.

iv. The variability in stock purchase due to the firm speculators purchase is another factor affecting working capital.

v.   The growth stage of the firm is another factor. A new growing firm will require a high level of Working Capital and the Working Capital cycle will be short and rapid.

vi. The credit policy of a firm can impact either negatively or positively upon its working capital. A liberal credit term will result in capital tie-up but a high level sales, and hence high level, while a tight credit policy may reduce sales but improve liquidity. Profitability may be low with high credit policy. Thus, the firm must strike a balance between liquidity and profitability.

vii. Another factor affecting the working capital of a firm is the extent to which short term funds (cash) are used to finance long term investment.

viii. An efficient operating cost will contribute to the working capital efficiency of a firm.

3.3 Operating Cycle

It is the total period of converting raw materials into cash and returning the cash into raw materials. This actually involves converting the raw materials to work in progress and the work in progress to finished good and the finished goods into sales and finally the sales to cash.
Figure 1 conversion cycle:

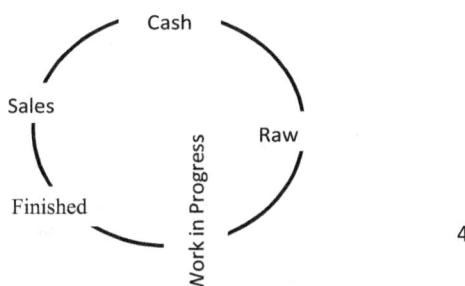

The operating cycle is the total period it will take to convert raw materials into cash as above.

To maintain an uninterrupted operating cycle, cash must be maintained. Liquidity is the most important factor for operating cycle.

3.3.1 Operating Cycle Length

To determine the length of operating cycle the total period of cash component of the operating cycle must be determined.

i.   **Inventory**

Raw materials conversion period $=$ $\dfrac{\text{Raw materials x 360}}{\text{Raw materials consumption}}$

Raw materials conversion $\dfrac{\text{RMI}}{\text{RMC}}$ x 360 (0r 365)

ii.   **Work In Progress**

Work in progress conversion period (WIPCP) =

$=$ $\dfrac{\text{Work in Progress Inventory}}{\text{Cost of Production}}$

$=$ $\dfrac{\text{W I P I}}{\text{Cost of production}}$ X 360 (or 365)

iii.   **Finished Goods**

$\dfrac{\text{Finished good conversion period (FGI)}}{\text{Cost of goods sold}}$ X 360 (or 365)

iv.   Book Debts Conversion Period (BDCP)
            (Debt repayment period)

       $=$ $\dfrac{\text{Book debt inventory}}{\text{Credit sales}}$ or $\dfrac{\text{Debtor}}{\text{Credit sales}}$ x 360(or 365)

v.   Payable Different Period
          (Credit Repayment Period)
          Creditors

Credit purchase x 360(or 365)

Illustration 1

The information below is extracted from the records of Chantel Plc.

	1998	1999	2000
Stock: Raw material	100,000	140,000	160,000
Work in progress	78,000	90,000	100,000
Finished goods	90, 000	128,000	160,000
Purchases	500,000	700,000	800,000
Cost of goods sold	800,000	900,000	980,000
Sales	800,000	1,900,000	1,200,000
Debtor	170,000	200,000	280,000
Trade creditors	90,000	100,000	120,000

Assume a 365 days year.

Compute: The operating cycle of the business.

SOLUTION

	1998 (Days)	1999 (Days)	2000 (Days)
Days taken can be computed as below.			
	1998	**1999**	**2000**
Raw material x 365 / Purchases	73	73	73
1-2 Trade creditor x 365 / Purchases	65.7	52.1	54.75
3-4 Word in progress x 365 / Cost of sales	35.59	36.5	37.24
4-5 Finished goods x 365 / Cost f sales	41.06	51.91	59.59
5-6 Debtors x 365 / Sales	68.94	66.97	85.17
(Total length of days)	284.29	280.48	309.75

3.4   Financing Working Capital

In financing working capital the risk return trading must be considered That is, the cost of fund and return from usage of that fund must be given a considerate attention, to ensure profitability and liquidity. Financing method must equally be flexible to accommodate constant change involved in working capital management. Thus there are three major methods of financing working capital namely:

1. *Long Term Financing:* This involves using fund from long term securities.
2. *Short Term Financing:* This involves using fund from short term securities.
3. *Spontaneous Financing:* This involve utilization of short term un-negotiated financing source e.g. credit from creditors.

4.0   SUMMARY

This unit examined working capital management. It also considered the factors affecting working capital as well as its major concepts. The operating cycle was equally examined.

5.0   CONCLUSION

Working capital is the life blood of an organization, it consists the liquidity flow as different from the profitability of the organization. A profitable but illiquid business could be forced to close down.

SELF-ASSESSMENT EXERCISE

1. What is working capital management?
2. Explain the major factors affecting working capital

6.0   TUTOR-MARKED ASSIGNMENT (TMAs)

1. Explain working capital management.
2. What are the factors affecting working capital?
3. What are gross concept and net concept?
4. Describe the operating cycle.

UNIT 4   CASH MANAGEMENT

CONTENTS

1.0   Introduction
2.0   Objectives
3.0   Main Content
        3.1 Cash Management
        3.2 Motives for Holding Cash
4.0   Conclusion
5.0   Summary
6.0   Tutor-Marked Assignment

1.0   INTRODUCTION

In the previous unit, we examined working capital management. And in this unit, we shall examine one of the components of working capital management – cash management and its related concepts.

2.0   OBJECTIVES

At the end of this unit, you should be able to:

• define cash management
• explain other concepts relating to cash management.

3.0   MAIN CONTENT

3.1   Cash Management

Cash is the most liquid assets of the company; it is used as a medium of exchange in business activities. No business can survive without it. Sales represent inflow of cash, while purchase brings about outflow of cash. It is used to meet daily components of organization obligations. Cash management involves three major stages namely: Cash planning, Cash flow management and maintaining optimal cash level.

Cash planning entails analyzing the organizational cash needed and estimating inflow and outflow of cash. The purpose is to avoid carrying excess cash or running into cash shortages.

Managing the cash flow involves evolving method of maximizing cash outflow. Keeping optimal cash level, no surplus cash or shortage of cash exist.

3.1.1 Cash Planning

This is a process of estimating current and future cash needs for the organization and making appropriate effort to attain these. The singular purpose of cash planning is to avoid excess liquid and low shortage of cash.

3.1.2 Cash Budgeting and Financing

Cash budgeting entails estimating relative inflow and outflow throughout the life of the asset. The cash budget could be long term or share term capital. A cash budget that goes beyond a year will be termed long term budget.

Illustration 1
Kingston Company produced the following information covering November, December, January, February, and March 2015. The information is stated below:

	NOV	DEC	JAN	FEB	MAR
	$	$	$	$	$
Sales	150,000	200,000	200,000	300,000	400,000
Expenses	10,000	12,000	12,000	13,000	15,000
Wages	15,000	16,000	18,000	20,000	25,000
Loan repay	10,000	10,000	10,000	10,000	10,000
Purchases	150,000	160,000	180,000	200,000	250,000
Rental income (Rec'd)	10,000	12,000		18000	20,000
	25,000				

Additional Information
Before preparing the cash budget, your enquiry revealed the following:

i.   Payment for sales is 50% cash sales and 50% credit sales. The credit sales are paid for in two equal installments a month after sales.
ii.   Purchases are paid for 40% in the month of purchases and the remaining are paid in two equal installments a month after purchase.

The management of Kingston Company has requested you to preparea cash budget for the firm covering January, February and March, 2011.

SOLUTION **CASH**
BUDGET

	January	February	March
	$	$	$
Sales	187,500	250,000	325,000
Rental Income	18,000	20,000	25,000
	205,500	270,000	350,000
Payment			
Purchases	(165,000)	(182,000)	(214,000)
Expenses	(12,000)	(13,000)	(15,000)
Wages	(18,000)	(20,000)	(25,000)
Loan repayment	(10,000)	(10.000)	(10,000)
	205,000	225,000	264,000
Balance	500	45,000	86,000
	205,500	270,000	350,000

WORKINGS

SALES

NOV	DEC	JAN	FEB	MAR
$	$	$	$	$
75,000	37,500	37,500		
------	100,000	50,000	50,000	

PURCHASES

NOV	DEC	JAN	FEB	MAR
$	$	$	$	$
60,000	45,000	45,000	-------	-------
--------	64,000	48,000	48,000	-------
--------	--------	72,000	54,000	54,000
--------	--------	---------	80,000	60,000
--------	--------	--------	--------	100,000
60,000	109,000	165,000	182,000	214,000

3.1.3 Managing the Cash Flows

This is a process of ensuring adequate cash collection period and the disbursement of the same. The purpose is to ensure accelerated cash collections and decelerated cash disbursements.

3.1.4 Cash Management Techniques

1. **Accelerated Cash Collections:** This is a method of ensuring reduction in time lag or gap between the time customers enjoys a service or buys a product and the time the customer receives the bill and settles it, and the time cash becomes available for maintaining the operating cycle.

    A cash collection method could either be centralized or decentralized system or the lock- box system. The lock-box system entails establishing various collections centres taking into account customer location and the volume of remittances.

2. **Optimal Cash Level:** This is determined through the use of Economic Order Quantity. It is used to determine the optimal cash level.

Formula: $EOQ = \sqrt{\dfrac{2DO}{C}}$

D = Cash need or cash demand
O = Cost of cash investment

C = Cost of carrying cash

Illustration 2

Khemite Plc operates a centralized collection system. It takes 6 days to receive mail remittance and another 3 days for processing mail. Khemite Plc daily collection amount to $600,000. Realtutu Plc currently is thinking about the introduction of Lock - Box System. By this same time mailing is expected to fall by two days while the processing time is also expected to drop by two days. Interest of 22% is expected to be paid by PEPZIM BANK PLC.

Required:
a) Find the fall in cash balance expected to result from adopting the lock-box.
b) What is the opportunity cost of the present centralized system?
c) Should the lock-box system be established if its annual cost is $100,000?

Solution
(a.)   Reduction in cash balances
       = Time saved X Daily Average Collection
       = 2 x 600,000 = $1,200,000
(b)   Opportunity Cost: Interest Rate X Reduction in Daily Cash Balance
       = 0.22 X 1200,000 = $264,000
(c)   Cost of lock Box System   = $100,000

The new system should be adopted since the lock box system cost less than the opportunity cost.

That's lock box system = $100,000
Opportunity Cost = $264,000

Illustration 3

Qabalat Plc required 100,000 annually for raw material purchases. This cost is equally available for lending at a cost of 30% annually. $200 transaction cost will be required to secure the cash required; Qabalat's Cash flow follows an annuity.

Required
(1)   Compute the optimal cash conversion size for Qabalat Plc.
(2)   Compute total cost of holding cash in hand during this period.
(3)   How often (in days) will cash conversion be made, assume a 30 days month.

Solution
(a)   **Using the EOQ Method**   = $(OCL) \sqrt{\dfrac{2DO}{}}$

Optimal Cash level   C
    Where D = Cash demand
            O = Holding cost
            C = Carry cost
(Carrying cost) all in capital letter

Cost in naira   = $\dfrac{100,000 \times 0.30}{\text{Cost} \quad \times \quad I}$ = $30,000

Cash Demand (year)   = $100,000

Carrying cost   = $\dfrac{30,000}{100,000} \times \dfrac{1}{12}$ =   0.025

Carrying cost = 0.025

OCL   = $\sqrt{\dfrac{2 \times 100,000 \times 200}{0.025}}$ =   40,000

b.   The cost of holding cash during the period is the opportunity cost
     of not investing cash = $\dfrac{030 \times 100,000 \times 30}{360}$ = 2,500

C.   Number of order = $\dfrac{100,000}{40,000}$ = 2.5 times

     The number of days = $\dfrac{360}{2.5}$

                                = 144 days

3.2   Motives for Holding Cash

Organization should hold cash for three purposes as follows:

i.   **Transactionary Motives**
     The business organization holds cash for the purpose of
     conducting its day to day activities such as for the purchase of raw
     materials, payment of wages and salaries, maintenance of machine
     etc.

ii. **Precautionary Motives**
     The business organization holds cash to meet unexpected
     contingencies. This acts as a 'buffer' to meet unexpected needs for
     cash.

iii. **Speculative Motives**
     Corporate organization may hold cash for the purpose of investing
     in business opportunities that may surface suddenly.

4.0   SUMMARY

This unit examined cash management component of the working capital management. It also considered others concepts relating to cash management as well as the motives for holding cash.

5.0   CONCLUSION

Cash is the most liquid assets of the company; it is used as a medium of exchange in business activities. No business can survive without it. Cash management involves three major stages namely: Cash planning, Cash flow management and maintaining optimal cash level.

Managing the cash flow involves evolving method of maximizing cash outflow, keeping optimal cash level, no surplus cash or shortage of cash exist.

6.0   TUTOR-MARKED ASSIGNMENT (TMAs)

1.   What is cash management?
2.   Explain the following concepts:
     a.   Cash planning
     b.   Cash budgeting and financing
3.   What are the cash management techniques?
4.   Mention the motives for holding cash?

UNIT 5   INVENTORY MANAGEMENT

CONTENTS

1.0   INTRODUCTION

In this unit, we shall examine another important component of working capital management i.e. inventory/stock management.

2.0   OBJECTIVES

At the end of this unit, you should be able to:

- define inventory/stock management
- enumerate and explain other concepts relating to inventory management
- explain EOQ and calculate it

3.0   MAIN CONTENT

3.1   Inventory Management

Inventory is stock. It includes raw materials, work in progress and finished goods ready for sales. It is the most illiquid component of the working capital. Thus a company willing to estimate its liquid must deduct the inventory or stock portion of the current asset before it against the current liability to obtain the quick asset ratio or the acid out Ratio. The formula for calculating working capital and Acid test ratios are:

Working Capital Ratio   =   Current Asset
                                Current liability
Acid test ratio   =   Current Asset - Stock

Current Liabilities

The firm must decide what quantity of stock is needed, at what point should order be made and at what price and what is the cost of stock out; can we reduce stock costs? These questions will help the financial manager to work out a proper stock management policy.

It is imperative to know that the firm can pile up stock in order to eliminate cost in production runs, sometimes they do keep large stock to reduce the time lag between when an inventory is needed and when t is fully bought.

3.1.1 Optimum Level of Stock

The economic order quantity (E.O.Q provides the firm with the most profitable form of obtaining the Optimum level of raw material.

$$E.O.Q = \sqrt{\frac{2DO}{C}}$$

Where D = Annual demand

O = Ordering cost   C = Carry cost

Ordering Cost: This is cost associated with placing new order such as invoices cost, book-keeping of inventory, cost of stationary, transportation cost and inspection handling cost.

Carrying Cost: Is the cost incurred to hold the stock. To protect the stock, such cost includes, storage cost, insurance, depreciation, cost of obsolescence and deterioration cost.

3.1.2 Minimum Stock Level (Margin of safety or buffer stock):

It is the level to which stock should not fall before new order is place it is the stock's margin of safety. It constitutes the firms buffer stock.

Minimum Stock Level: Re-order level - (Normal consumption X Average reorder period).

Maximum Stock Level: This is the highest level stock must not rise above. It is the level above which stock should not rise.

Maximum Stock Level =

Reorder Level - (Min consumption x minimum reorder period) + Reorder quantity.

ROL - (Min consumption x min reorder period) + ROQ.

Illustration 1

Mary James Ltd uses a particular component at a rate of 48,000 per annum. These are obtained from an external supplier at a basic cost of $50k each. Replenishment orders can be obtained promptly, though it entails sending a man and a lorry to collect the components, this would cost $40, this is assumed to be the only cost of ordering.

The storage cost of stock is 15% of the cost of the component.
You are required to:

(a)   Calculate the EOQ

SOLUTION

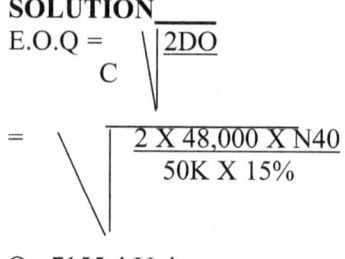

$$E.O.Q = \sqrt{\frac{2DO}{C}}$$

$$= \sqrt{\frac{2 \times 48,000 \times N40}{50K \times 15\%}}$$

Q =7155.4 Units

4.0   CONLUSION

This unit examined inventory management and its components. Economic order quantity (EOQ) was equally given adequate attention.

5.0   SUMMARY

Inventory management – an important component of working capital management – also known as stock includes raw materials, work in progress and finished goods ready for sales. It is the most non-liquid component of the working capital.

6.0   TUTOR-MARKED ASSIGNMENT

1.   Define stock management
2.   What is maximum stock level?
3.   What is minimum stock level?
4.   Briefly

UNIT 6   ACCOUNT RECEIVABLES AND PAYABLES

CONTENTS

1.0   Introduction
2.0   Objectives
3.0   Main Content
    3.1   Management of Creditors (Account Payable)
    3.2   Management of Debtors (Account Receivable)
    3.3   Factors influencing Credit Control Policy
    3.4   Factors to be considered in granting Credit to a Specific
           Customer
4.0   Conclusion
5.0   Summary
6.0   Tutor-Marked Assignment

1.0   INTRODUCTION

In this unit, we shall examine the management of debtors and creditors i.e.
accounts receivable and payable. Also, the factors influencing credit control
as well as the factors to be considered in granting credits to customers shall
be considered.

2.0   OBJECTIVES

At the end of this unit, you should be able to:

- explain account receivable and payable
- state the factors influencing credit control policy
- mention the factors to be considered in granting credits to customers

3.0   MAIN CONTENT

3.1   Management of Creditors (Account Payable)

This is a source of fund to the firm. It constitutes the cheapest source of
fund to the firm; however, the firm must design a proper method of
settling the creditors. This will enhance continuous and repeated purchase.
Creditors include the accounts payable where the credit is on overdraft,
then the cost of the overdraft must be considered and compared with cost
of alternative financing.

3.2 Management of Debtors (Account Receivable)

The Debtor includes accounts receivable. It is very important to the firm due to the fact that such debtor could impact negatively on the liquidity of the firm. Liquidity of the firm accounts for the viability of such firm's security. The debtor is a tied down capital, this capital tied down would impact negatively on the firm's ability to finance other current assets.

Thus the firm must establish a flexible credit policy. Sometimes the credit Policy of a firm might be rigid depending on the nature of the business, the Current Asset Stock and the preference for liquidity over profitability. Thus the Credit Policy of the firm should be flexible enough to boost profitability of the firm. It is also important to consider liquidity as the daily activities of the firm need cash realized from sale to meet the needs for finance for the moment.

3.3 Factors Influencing Credit Control Policy

i. **Policy of the competitors:** The Credit Control Policy of the competitors is of utmost important in deciding a company Credit policy; since Credit Policy have direct impact on sales such that the higher the credit granted the higher the sales; Thus a competitor offering a hot credit facility {say 90 days} will be considered to have more sales than a company with less credit facility (say 30 days).

ii. **Nature of Product:** A company with a unique product, without substitute will not need to consider any credit policy. A monopoly will not consider any credit facility nor have any credit policy.

iii. **Trade-Off between Profits on Sales and Cost of Having Debtors Plus Bad Debts:**

Increased profits anticipated from increased sales coming in a result of credit facility should be compared with cost of bad debt and maintenance cost of a wage credit control department before deciding on a particular credit policy.

iv. **Customers Risk Category:** The customers risk category should be considered in grating credit facility. Customer with poor record of credit repayment will have less chance of obtaining credit facility compare compared with a customer with good record of credit repayment.

v. **Cost of Debt Factoring and Invoice Discounting:** The cost involved in debt factoring and invoice discounting should be given congruence in granting credit facilities. Where the cost of factoring is too high, it becomes difficult therefore, to grant credit facilities.

vi. **Cost of Working Capital:** The financial cost of working capital should be considered. The increased working capital required should be considered in term of cost involved and risk thereon.

3.4 Factors to be considered in Granting Credit to a Specific Customer

i. **Trade Reference:** One or more companies which the customer has dealt with in business before will be asked to give a reference on the Customer.

ii. **Bank reference or bank's opinion:** A bank may also be asked to comment on the financial standing of its customers.

iii. **Published information:** e.g. annual accounts of the particular customer can be analyzed to determine its liquidity and profitability position.

iv. **Salesmen's Opinion:** The opinion of the salesmen should be considered when granting credit facility to a customer since they are more close to the customer than others.

iv. **Customers Past Credit Record:** An emanation of how will the customer has paid in the past might give some insight as to how well he will perform in the future.

4.0 SUMMARY

In this unit, we examined the working capital management components i.e. debtors and creditor management, the factors affecting working capital. It outlined the factors Influencing Credit Control Policy and the factors to be considered in granting credit to a specific customer.

5.0 CONCLUSION

The management of creditors and debtors is very crucial in any business organization. And considerable factors should be looked into when granting credit to customers.

SELF-ASSESSMENT EXERCISE

Explain the factors influencing credit control policy.

6.0   TUTOR-MARKED ASSIGNMENT (TMAs)

1.   What is account receivable?
2.   Explain 'management of creditors'
3.   Mention the factors to be considered in granting credits to customers

MODULE 3

UNIT 1   ANALYSIS AND INTERPRETATION OF BASIC FINANCIAL STATEMENT

CONTENTS

1.0   Introduction
2.0   Objectives
3.0   Main Content
    3.1   Meaning and Definition of Financial Statement
4.0   Conclusion
5.0   Summary
6.0   Tutor-Marked Assignment

1.0   INTRODUCTION

A financial statement is an official document of the firm, which explores the entire financial information of the firm. The main aim of the financial statement is to provide information and understand the financial aspects of the firm. Hence, preparation of the financial statement is important as much as the financial decisions. Its analysis and interpretation are therefore crucial in any business organization.

Financial statements provide business owners with the basic tools for determining how well their operations perform at all times. Many entrepreneurs do not realize that financial statements have a value that goes beyond their use as supporting documents to loan applications and tax returns.

These statements are concise reports designed to summarize financial activities for specific periods. Owners and managers can use financial statement analysis to evaluate the past and current financial condition of their business, diagnose any existing financial problems, and forecast future trends in the firm's financial position.

It is the light of the above that this unit examines the analysis and interpretation of financial statement of business organizations.

2.0   OBJECTIVES

At the end of this unit, you should be to:

* define financial statement
* analyze and interpret basic financial statement.

3.0   MAIN CONTENT

3.1   Meaning and Definition of Financial Statement

According to Hamptors John, the financial statement is an organized collection of data according to logical and consistent accounting procedures. Its purpose is to convey an understanding of financial aspects of a business firm. It may show a position at a moment of time as in the case of a balance-sheet or may reveal a service of activities over a given period of time, as in the case of an income statement.

Financial statements are the summary of the accounting process, which provides useful information to both internal and external parties. John N. Nyer also defines it "Financial statements provide a summary of the accounting of a business enterprise, the balance-sheet reflecting the assets, liabilities and capital as on a certain data and the income statement showing the results of operations during a certain period".

This unit provides you with a basic understanding of the components and purposes of financial statements. The Balance Sheet and Income Statement formats are designed as general models and are not complete for every business operation. Computation of income for financial accounting purposes is done according to the rules of Generally Accepted Accounting Principles (known as GAAP).

Financial statements generally consist of two important statements

(i)   the income statement or profit and loss account.
(ii)   the position statement.

A part from that, the business concern also prepares some of the other parts of statements, which are very useful to the internal purpose such as:

(i)   Statement of changes in owner's equity.
(ii)   Statement of changes in financial position.

3.1.1 Income Statement

Income statement is also called as profit and loss account, which reflects the operational position of the firm during a particular period. Normally it consists of one accounting year.

It determines the entire operational performance of the concern like total revenue generated and expenses incurred for earning that revenue.
Income statement helps to ascertain the gross profit and net profit of the concern.

Gross profit is determined by preparation of trading or manufacturing a/c and net profit is determined by preparation of profit and loss account.
The following terms are commonly found on an income statement:

i.   **Heading**
        The first facts to appear on any statement are the legal name of the business, the type of statement, and the period of time reported, e.g., month, quarter, or year.

ii.   **Column Headings**
        If you include both current month and year-to-date columns on the Income Statement you can review trends from accounting period to accounting period and compare previous similar periods. Also, it is often helpful to show the dollar amounts as percentages of net sales. This helps you analyze performance and compare your company to similar businesses. Remember, you can choose any period of time to analyze.

iii.   **Revenue**
        All income flowing into a business for services rendered or goods sold comes under this category. In addition to actual cash transactions, the revenue figure reflects amounts due from customers on accounts receivable as well as equivalent cash values for merchandise or other tangible items used as payment.

iv.   **Less Sales Returns and Allowances**
        The value of returned merchandise and allowances made for defective goods must be subtracted from gross sales to determine net sales.

v.   **Cost of Goods Sold**
        Cost of goods sold equals the amount of goods available for sale minus the inventory remaining at the end of the accounting period. (Total goods available = beginning inventory + cost of purchasing or manufacturing new merchandise during the accounting period). Cost of goods sold includes all costs directly related to the

production of the product invoiced during the accounting period. Service businesses generally have no cost of goods sold.

vi. **Gross Profit**

Also called *gross margin*, this figure is the difference between the cost of goods sold and net sales (Net Sales - Cost of Goods Sold = Gross Profit). It is the business's profit before operating expenses and taxes.

vii. **Operating Expenses**

The expenses of conducting business operations generally fall into two broad categories: selling and general administrative. Manufacturers normally include some operating expenses, such as machinery and labor depreciation, as part of cost of sales.

viii. **Total (Net) Operating Income**

Total operating expenses are subtracted from gross profit to show what the business earned before financial revenue and expenses, taxes, and extraordinary items.

ix. **Other Revenue and Expenses**

Income and expenses that are not generated by the usual operations of a business and that are not considered extraordinary (see Item 11) are recorded here. Typically included in this category are financial revenue, such as interest from investments, and financial expenses, such as interest on borrowed capital. (Loan principal is not considered an expense. It is a liability and is listed as such on the Balance Sheet).

x. **Pretax Income**

To derive this figure, also called pretax profit, total financial revenue (minus total financial expenses) is added to total operating income. Taxes are subtracted from pretax income if the business is a 'C' corporation. Proprietorships, limited liability companies, and 'S' corporations do not pay business taxes on income; the income is reported on the owners' personal returns. (For tax planning purposes, accountants estimate the annual taxes due, then project the monthly portion.)

xi. **Extraordinary Gain [Loss] Net of Income Tax [Benefit]**

Within the framework of an individual business type and location, any occurrence that is highly unusual in nature, could not be foreseen, is not expected to recur, and that generates income or causes a loss is considered an extraordinary item. The extraordinary gain or loss is shown after calculating tax liability (or tax benefit, as would be the case with an extraordinary loss) on the Income Statement. Examples: A court award to a business not previously involved in lawsuits would be an extraordinary gain; a major casualty would be an extraordinary loss.

xii.   **Net Income**
         Also called net profit, this figure represents the sum of all expenses
         (including taxes, if applicable). Net income or profit is commonly
         referred to as the *bottom line*.
xiii.   **Earnings per Share**
         Total outstanding common stock (the number of shares currently
         owned by stockholders) is divided into net income to derive this
         figure. It is not applicable to proprietorships and limited liability
         companies, but must be shown on the Income Statements of all
         publicly held corporations.

3.1.2 Position Statement

Position statement is also called as balance sheet, which reflects the
financial position of the firm at the end of the financial year.

Position statement helps to ascertain and understand the total assets,
liabilities and capital of the firm. One can understand the strength and
weakness of the concern with the help of the position statement.

The following terms are commonly found on a balance sheet:

i.   **Heading**
        The legal name of the business, the type of statement, and the day,
        month, and year must be shown at the top of the report.
ii.   **Assets**
        Anything of value that is owned or legally due the business is
        included under this heading.   Total assets include all net realizable
        and net book (also called net carrying) values. Net realizable and net
        book values are amounts derived by subtracting from the acquisition
        price of assets any estimated allowances for doubtful accounts,
        depreciation, and amortization, such as amortization of a premium
        during the term of an insurance policy. Appreciated values are not
        usually considered on Balance Sheets, except, for example, when
        you are recording stock portfolio values.
iii.   **Current Assets**
        Cash and resources that can be converted into cash within 12 months
        of the date of the financial position (or during one established cycle
        of operations) are considered current. Besides cash (money on hand
        and demand deposits in the bank, such as regular savings accounts
        and checking accounts), these resources include the items listed
        below. They are ranked in a generally accepted order of decreasing
        liquidity--that is, the ease with which the items could be converted to

cash. The items that appear on the financial position of an organization include:

a. **Accounts Receivable:** The amounts due from customers in payment for merchandise or services.

b. **Inventory:** Includes raw materials on hand, work in process, and all finished goods either manufactured or purchased for resale. Inventory value is based on unit cost and is calculated by any of several methods (see Inventory Valuation below).

c. **Temporary Investments:** Interest- yielding or dividend-yielding holdings expected to be converted into cash within a year. Also called *marketable securities* or *short-term investments*, they include certificates of deposit, stocks and bonds, and time deposit savings accounts. According to accounting principles, they must be listed on the financial position at either their original cost or their market value, whichever is less.

d. Prepaid Expenses: Goods, benefits, or services a business pays for in advance of use. Examples are insurance protection, floor space and office supplies.

e. **Long-Term Investments**
Also called long-term assets, these resources are holdings that the business intends to keep for a year or longer and that typically yield interest or dividends. Included are stocks, bonds and savings accounts earmarked for special purposes.

f. **Fixed Assets**
Fixed assets, frequently called plant and equipment, are the resources a business owns or acquires for use in operations and does not intend to resell. Regardless of current market value, land is listed at its original purchase price, with no allowance for appreciation or depreciation. Other fixed assets are listed at cost, minus depreciation. Fixed assets may be leased rather than owned. Depending on the leasing arrangement, both the value and liability of the leased property may need to be listed on the Balance Sheet.

g. **Other Assets**
Resources not listed with any of the above assets are grouped here. Examples include tangibles, such as outdated equipment which can be sold to the scrap yard, and intangibles, such as goodwill, trademarks and patents.

h. **Liabilities**
This term covers all monetary obligations of a business and all claims creditors have on its assets.

i.   Current Liabilities

All debts and obligations payable within 12 months or within one cycle of operations are detailed here. Typically, they include the following, which generally are listed in the order due:

Accounts Payable: Amounts owed to suppliers for goods and service purchased in connection with business operations.

i.   Short-Term Debt: The balances of principal due to pay off short-term debt for borrowed funds.

ii.   Current Portion of Long-Term Debt: Current amount due of total balance on notes whose terms exceed 12 months.

iii.   Interest Payable: Any accrued amounts due for use of both short-and long-term borrowed capital and credit extended to the business.

iv.   Taxes Payable: Amounts estimated by an accountant to have been incurred during the accounting period. For accounting purposes, this total may differ from the actual tax total required by the Internal Revenue Codes, since taxes payable are based on accounting income and not taxable income. (**Note:** Income taxes are business obligations for corporations; proprietorships and partnerships do not pay income taxes; the income is reported on the owners' personal returns.)

v.   Accrued Payroll: Salaries and wages currently owed but not yet paid.

j.   Long Term Liabilities

Long-term liabilities are notes, payments, or mortgage payments due over a period exceeding 12 months or one cycle of operations. They are listed by outstanding balance (minus the Current Portion due).

k.   Equity

Also called net worth, equity is the claim of the owner(s) on the assets of the business. In a proprietorship or limited liability company, equity is each owner's original investment, plus any earnings after withdrawals.

In a corporation, the owners are the shareholders--those who have invested capital (cash or other assets) in exchange for shares of stock. The corporation's equity is the sum of contributions plus earnings retained after paying dividends. It is detailed as follows:

i.   **Capital Stock:** The total amount invested in the business in exchange for shares of stock at value up to the par value. Par is the per-share price assigned to the original issue of stock, regardless of subsequent selling prices.

ii.   **Capital Paid-In in Excess of Par:** The amount in excess of par value that a business receives from shares of stock sold at a value above par.

iii.   **Treasury Stock:** When a company buys back its own stock or when a closely held business buys out other owners. The value of the stock is recorded here and ordinarily does not receive dividends.

iv.   **Retained Earnings:** The total accumulated net income minus the total accumulated dividends declared since the corporation's founding. These earnings are part of the total equity for any business. However, the figure is usually listed separately from owner investments only on corporate Balance Sheets which are done for the benefit of shareholders.

I.   **Total Liabilities and Equity**

The sum of these two amounts must always equal Total Assets.

3.1.3 Reconciliation of Equity

This statement reconciles the equity shown on the current Balance Sheet. For corporations this statement is referred to as the Statement of Retained Earnings or Statement of Shareholder Equity. For limited liability companies it is referred to as the Statement of Members Equity and for Proprietorships as the Statement of Owner's Equity. It records equity at the beginning of the accounting period and details additions to, or subtractions from, this amount made during the period. Additions and subtractions typically are net income or loss and owner contributions and/or deductions. Figures used to compile this statement are derived from previous and current Balance Sheets and from the current Income Statement.

3.1.4 Statement of Cash Flows

The fourth main document of financial reporting is the Statement of Cash Flows. Many small business owners and managers find that the cash flow statement is perhaps the most useful of all the financial statements for planning purposes. Cash is the life blood of a small business – if the business runs out of cash chances are good that the business is out of business. This is because most small businesses do not have the ability to borrow money as easily as larger business can.

The statement can be prepared frequently (monthly, quarterly) and is a valuable tool that summarizes the relationship between the Balance Sheet and the Income Statement and traces the.

In **financial accounting,** a cash flow statement, also known as *statement of cash flows* or *funds flow statement,* is a **financial statement** that shows how changes in financial position and income affect **cash and cash equivalents**, and breaks the analysis down to operating, investing, and financing activities. Essentially, the cash flow statement is concerned with the flow of cash in and cash out of the business. The statement captures both the current operating results and the accompanying changes in the balance sheet. As an analytical tool, the statement of cash flows is useful in determining the short-term viability of a company, particularly its ability to pay bills.

By understanding the amounts and causes of changes in cash balances, the entrepreneur can realistically budget for continued business operations and growth. For example, the Statement of Cash Flows helps answer such questions as: Will present working capital allow the business to acquire new equipment, or will financing be necessary?

Many small businesses may not need to prepare the Statement of Cash Flows. However, according to GAAP, it should be prepared whenever an operation's financial statements are compiled, reviewed, or audited by a CPA. In addition, creditors, investors, new owners or partners, and the Internal Revenue Service may require the information it provides. This statement can usually be produced by most accounting software applications.

3.1.5 Statement of Changes in Owner's Equity

It is also called as statement of retained earnings. This statement provides information about the changes or position of owner's equity in the company. How the retained earnings are employed in the business concern. Nowadays, preparation of this statement is not popular and nobody is going to prepare the separate statement of changes in owner's equity.

3.1.6 Statement of Changes in Financial Position

Income statement and position statement shows only about the position of the finance; hence it can't measure the actual position of the financial statement. Statement of changes in financial position helps to understand the changes in financial position from one period to another period.

Statement of changes in financial position involves two important areas such as fund flow statement which involves the changes in working capital position and cash flow statement which involves the changes in cash position.

3.1.7 Notes to Financial Statements

If an important factor does not fit into the regular categories of a financial statement, it should be included as a note. Also, anything that might affect the financial position of a business must be documented. Three major types of notes include:

1. **Methodology**
    Discussion of the accounting principles used by the company. For example, accrual basis of accounting vs. cash basis of accounting.
    Contingent Liabilities
    Circumstances that have occurred as of the statement date and which represent potential financial obligations must be recorded by type and estimated amount. Example: A business owner cosigns a bank note. If the primary borrower should default, the business owner who cosigned would become liable.
2. **Required Disclosures**
    It is necessary that all significant information about the company be described in a disclosure statement. Example: If the business has changed accounting procedures since the last accounting period, the change must be described.

3.1.8 Financial Ratios

Financial ratios are a valuable and easy way to interpret the numbers found in statements. Ratio analysis provides the ability to understand the relationship between figures on spreadsheets. It can help you to answer critical questions such as whether the business is carrying excess debt or inventory, whether customers are paying according to terms, and whether the operating expenses are too high.

When computing financial relationships, a good indication of the company's financial strengths and weaknesses becomes clear. Examining these ratios over time provides some insight as to how effectively the business is being operated.

Many industries compile average (or standard) industry ratios each year. Standard or average industry ratios offer the small business owner a means of comparing his or her company with others within the same industry. In this manner they provide yet another measurement of an individual company's strengths or weaknesses. RMA (Risk Management Association, formerly named Robert Morris & Associates) is a good source of comparative financial ratios.

Following are the most critical ratios for most businesses, though there are others that may be computed.

1.   Liquidity
Measures a company's capacity to pay its debts as they come due. There are two ratios for evaluation liquidity.

Current Ratio - Gauges how able a business is to pay current liabilities by using current assets only. Also called the *working capital ratio.* A general rule of thumb for the current ratio is 2 to 1 (or 2:1, or 2/1). However, an industry average may be a better standard than this rule of thumb.   The actual quality and management of assets must also be considered.

The formula is: **Total Current Assets**
                              Total Current Liabilities

Quick Ratio - Focuses on immediate liquidity (i.e., cash, accounts receivable, etc.) but specifically ignores inventory. Also called the *acid test ratio*, it indicates the extent to which you could pay current liabilities without relying on the sale of inventory. *Quick assets* are highly liquid-- those immediately convertible to cash. A rule of thumb states that, generally, your ratio should be 1 to 1 (or 1:1, or 1/1).
The formula is: **Cash + Accounts Receivable =**
                                        (+ any other quick assets)
                                        Current Liabilities

2.   Safety
Indicates a company's vulnerability to risk that is the degree of protection provided for the business' debt. Three ratios help you evaluate safety:

Debt to Worth - Also called *debt to net worth.* The Quantifies is relationship between the capital invested by owners, investors and the funds provided by creditors. The higher the ratio, the greater the risk to a current or future creditor. A lower ratio means your company is more financially stable and is probably in a better position to borrow now and in the future. However, an extremely low ratio may indicate that you are too conservative and are not letting the business realize its potential.

The formula is: **Total Liabilities (or Debt)**
                    Net Worth (or Total Equity)

Times Interest Earned – Assesses the company's ability to meet interest payments. It also evaluates the capacity to take on more debt. The higher the ratio the greater the company's ability to make its interest payments, perhaps take on more debt.

The formula is: **Earnings Before Interest & Taxes**
                    Interest Charges

Cash Flow to Current Maturity of Long-Term Debt - Indicates how well traditional cash flow (net profit plus depreciation) covers the company's debt principal payments due in the next 12 months. It also indicates if the company's cash flow can support additional debt.

The formula is: **Net Profit + Non-Cash Expenses***
                    Current Portion of Long-Term Debt

•   Such as depreciation, amortization, and depletion.

3.   Profitability

This measures the company's ability to generate a return on its resources. Use the following four ratios to help you answer the question, "Is my company as profitable as it should be?" An increase in the ratios is viewed as a positive trend.

Gross Profit Margin - Indicates how well the company can generate a return at the gross profit level. It addresses three areas: inventory control, pricing, and production efficiency.

The formula is: **Gross Profit**
                    Total Sales

Net Profit Margin - Shows how much net profit is derived from every dollar of total sales. It indicates how well the business has managed its operating expenses. It also can indicate whether the business is generating enough sales volume to cover minimum fixed costs and still leave an acceptable profit.

The formula is: **Net Profit**
                    Total Sales

Return on Assets - Evaluates how effectively the company employs its assets to generate a return. It measures efficiency.
     The formula is: **Net Profit**
                         Total Assets

Return on Net Worth - Also called *return on investment (ROI)*, determines the rate of return on the invested capital. It is used to compare investment in the company against other investment opportunities, such as stocks, real estate, savings, etc. There should be a direct relationship between ROI and risk (i.e., the greater the risk, the higher the return).

The formula is: **Net Profit**
                    Net Worth

4.   Efficiency

Evaluates how well the company manages its assets. Besides determining the value of the company's assets, you should also analyze how effectively the company employs its assets. You can use the following ratios:

Accounts Receivable Turnover - Shows the number of times accounts receivable are paid and reestablished during the accounting period. The higher the turnover, the faster the business is collecting its receivables and the more cash the company generally has on hand.
The formula is: **Total Net Sales**
                    Average Accounts Receivable

Accounts Receivable Collection Period - Reveals how many days it takes to collect all accounts receivable. As with accounts receivable turnover (above), fewer days means the company is collecting more quickly on its accounts.

The formula is: **365 Days**
                    Accounts Receivable Turnover

Accounts Payable Turnover - Shows how many times in one accounting period the company turns over (repays) its accounts payable to creditors. A higher number indicates either that the business has decided to hold on to its money longer, or that it is having greater difficulty paying creditors.

The formula is: **Cost of Goods Sold**
                    Average Accounts Payable

Payable Period - Shows how many days it takes to pay accounts payable. This ratio is similar to accounts payable turnover (above.) The business may be losing valuable creditor discounts by not paying promptly.

The formula is: **365 Days**
                    Accounts Payable Turnover

Inventory Turnover - Shows how many times in one accounting period the company turns over (sells) its inventory. This ratio is valuable for spotting understocking, overstocking, obsolescence, and the need for merchandising improvement.   Faster turnovers are generally viewed as a positive trend; they increase cash flow and reduce warehousing and other related costs. Average inventory can be calculated by averaging the inventory figure from the monthly Balance Sheets. In a cyclical business, this is especially important since there can be wide swings in asset levels during the year. For example, many retailers might have extra stock in October and November in preparation for the Thanksgiving and winter holiday sales.

The formula is: **Cost of Goods Sold**
                    Average Inventory

Inventory Turnover in Days - Identifies the average length of time in days it takes the inventory to turn over.   As with inventory turnover (above), fewer days mean that inventory is being sold more quickly.
The formula is: **365 Days**
                    Inventory Turnover

Sales to Net Worth - Indicates how many sales dollars are generated with each dollar of investment (net worth). This is a volume ratio.
The formula is: **Total Sales**
                    Average Net Worth

Sales to Total Assets - Indicates how efficiently the company generates sales on each dollar of assets. A volume indicator, this ratio measures the ability of the company's assets to generate sales.
The formula is: **Total Sales**
                    Average Total Assets

Debt Coverage Ratio - Is an indication of the company's ability to satisfy its debt obligations and its capacity to take on additional debt without impairing its survival.

The formula is: **Net Profit + Any Non-Cash Expenses**
Principal on Debt

3.1.8.1   Summary Table of Financial Ratios

Figure 1, Summary Table of Financial Ratios, shows several ratios that are commonly used for analyzing financial statements. Keep in mind that the ratios shown in Figure 1 are only a sample of dozens of widely-used ratios in financial statement analysis. Many of the ratios overlap.

Figure 1. Summary Table of Financial Ratios

Ratio	Formula	What it measures	What it tells you
Owners: Return on Investment (ROI)	Net Income / Average Owners' Equity	Return on owners' capital When compared with return on assets, it measures the extent to which financial leverage is being used for or against the owner.	How well is this company doing as an investment?
Return on Assets (ROA)	Net Income / Average Total Assets	How well assets have been employed by management.	How well has management employed company assets? Does it pay to borrow?
Managers: Net Profit Margin	Net Income / Sales	Operating efficiency. The ability to create sufficient profits from operating activities.	Are profits high enough, given the level of sales?
Asset Turnover	Sales /	Relative	How well are

	Average Total Assets	efficiency in using total resources to product output.	assets being used to generate sales revenue?
Return on Assets	$\dfrac{\text{Net Income}}{\text{Sales}}$ x $\dfrac{\text{Sales}}{\text{Total Assets}}$	Earning power on all assets; ROA ratio broken into its logical parts: turnover and margin.	How well has management employed company assets?
Average Collection Period	$\dfrac{\text{Average A/R x 365}}{\text{Annual Credit Sales}}$	Liquidity of receivables in terms of average number of days receivables are outstanding.	Are receivables coming in too slowly?
Inventory Turnover	$\dfrac{\text{Cost of Goods Sold Expense}}{\text{Average Inventory}}$	Liquidity of inventory; the number of times it turns over per year.	Is too much cash tied up in inventories?
Average Age of Payables	$\dfrac{\text{Average A/P x 365}}{\text{Net Purchases}}$	Approximate length of time a firm takes to pay its bills for trade purchases.	How quickly does a prospective customer pay its bills?
Short-Term Creditors Working Capital	Current Assets – Current Liabilities	Short-term debt-paying ability.	Does this customer have sufficient cash or other liquid assets to cover its short-term obligations?
Current Ratio	$\dfrac{\text{Current Assets}}{\text{Current Liabilities}}$	Short-term debt-paying ability without regard to	Does this customer have sufficient cash or

		the liquidity of current assets.	other liquid assets to cover its short-term obligations?
Quick Ratio	$\dfrac{\text{Cash+Mktble Sec.+A/R}}{\text{Current Liabilities}}$	Short-term debt-paying ability without having to rely on sale of inventory.	Does this customer have sufficient cash or other liquid assets to cover its short-term obligations?
Long-Term Creditors: Debt-to-Equity Ratio	$\dfrac{\text{Total Debt}}{\text{Total Equity}}$	Amount of assets provided by creditors for each dollar of assets provided by owner(s)	Is the company's debt load excessive?
Times Interest Earned)	$\dfrac{\text{Net Income+(Interest}}{\text{Interest Expense}}$	Ability to pay fixed charges for interest from operating profits.	earnings and cash flows sufficient to cover interest payments and some principal repayments?
Cash Flow to Liabilities	$\dfrac{\text{Operating Cash Flow}}{\text{Total Liabilities}}$	Total debt coverage. General debt-paying ability.	Are earnings and cash flows sufficient to cover interest payments and some principal repayments

Illustration 1

To illustrate financial statement analysis, we will use the financial statements of K-L Fashions, Inc. K-L Fashions is a direct mail order company for quality "cut and sewn" products. Their financial statements are presented in Figure 2. Like most small businesses, they have a relatively simple capital structure and their income statement reflects typical revenues and expenses. Inventory consists primarily of merchandise obtained under contract from approved garment makers and held for resale. K-L Fashions uses trade credit for purchases, but its sales consist almost entirely of credit card sales. Consequently, we see a very low accounts receivable balance compared with accounts payable. Some of the items that would normally be seen on financial statements have been consolidated to simplify the presentations.

Financial statement analysis can be applied from two different directions. Vertical analysis is the application of financial statement analysis to one set of financial statements. Here, we look "up and down" the statements for signs of strengths and weaknesses. Horizontal analysis looks at financial statements and ratios over time. In horizontal analysis, we look for trends -- whether the numbers are increasing or decreasing; whether particular components of the company's financial position are getting better or worse.

We will look at the financials from the perspectives of four different groups: owners, managers, short-term creditors and long-term credit on

Figure 2. K-L Fashions, Inc.

Income Statement for the year ended January 31:

(Naira in thousands)	2005	2004	2003	2002
Net Sales	$6,039,750	$5,452,010	$4,558,060	$3,362,910
Cost of Goods	3,573,070	3,135,730	2,616,710	1,903,480
Gross Profit	2,466,680	2,316,280	1,941,350	1,459,430
Selling, General and Administrative Expenses (including depreciation)	2,221,540	1,849,100	1,434,860	1,076,990
Income from Operations	245,140	467,180	506,490	382,440
Other Income (expenses):				
Interest and other income	14,470	19,510	27,250	14,410
Interest Expense	(10,180)	(13,990)	(12,320)	(13,570)
Income Before Income Taxes	249,430	472,700	521,420	383,280
Income Tax Provision	102,000	181,990	198,600	162,080
Net Income	$147,430	$290,710	$322,820	$221,200

(As a Percentage of Sales)

Net Sales	100.0%	100.0%	100.0%	100.0%
Cost of Goods	59.2	57.5	57.4	56.6
Gross Profit	40.8	42.5	42.6	43.4
Selling, General and Administrative Expenses (including depreciation)	36.8	33.9	31.5	32.0
Income from Operations	4.0	8.6	11.1	11.4
Other Income (expenses):				
Interest and other income	.3	.4	.6	.4
Interest Expense	(.2)	(.3)	(.3)	(.4)
Income Before Income Taxes	4.1	8.7	11.4	11.4
Income Tax Provision	1.7	3.4	4.3	4.8
Net Income	2.4%	5.3%	7.1%	6.6%

Figure 2. (Cont.) K-L Fashions, Inc.
Financial position as at January 31:

(Naira in thousands)	2005	2004	2003	2002
Assets				
Current Assets:				
Cash and Cash Equivalents	$272,640	$82,540	$321,390	$281,750
Receivables	12,090	3,480	7,550	2,740
Inventory	738,630	857,090	668,200	464,440
Prepaid Expenses	54,880	54,030	39,670	33,630
Total Current Assets	1,078,240	997,140	1,036,810	782,560
Property, Plant & Equipment (at cost):				
Land and Buildings	531,270	383,350	312,670	151,140
Fixtures and equipment	476,460	411,230	251,920	219,740

79

Leasehold improvements		15,120		9,080
	16,460		12,340	
Construction in progress	----	46,370		6,740
			32,800	
Less Accumulated Depreciation				
	(248,430)	(183,890)	(135,020)	(99,470)
Property, Plant & Equipment, net				
	775,760	672,180	474,710	287,230
Total Assets	$1,854,0 00	$1,669,32 0	$1,511,5 20	$1,069,79 0

Liabilities and Stockholders' Equity				
Current Liabilities:				
Accounts Payable				
	$377,970	$244,150	$259,040	$212,223
Advance Payment on Orders		2,030		4,530
	4,460		3,500	
Income Taxes Payable		53,020		53,940
	70,800		103,970	
Other Current Obligations		139,950		
	154,510		148,790	117,900
Total Current Liabilities		439,150		
	607,740		515,300	388,600
Long-Term Debt	78,000	84,130	76,740	86,670
Stockholders' Equity:				
Common Stock; 20.1M, 20.1M &20.0M		2,010		2,000
Shares, respectively, at par	2,010		2,000	
Additional Capital, net		307,810		
	311,360		293,080	223,080
Retained Earnings		875,160		
	983,810		624,400	341,666
Less Treasury Stock, at cost			----	----
	(128,920)	(38,940)		
Total Stockholders' Equity		1,146,040		
	1,168,260		919,480	566,740
Total Liabilities and Equity	$1,854,0 00	$1,669,32 0	$1,511,5 20	$1,069,79 0

Figure 2. K-L Fashions, Inc.

Statement of Cash Flows
(Major component totals only)
For the year ended January 31:
(Naira in thousands)

	2005	2004	2003	2001
Net cash flows from operating activities	$512,020	$95,200	$255,600	$217,030
Net cash flows from investing activities	(175,410)	(250,560)	(226,690)	(52,310)
Net cash flows from financing activities	(146,510)	(83,490)	10,730	(43,290)
Net increase (decrease) In cash and cash equivalents	$ 190,100	$(238,850)	$39,640	$121,430

Analyzing the Financials from Four Different Groups

(a) Owners

Although owners of small businesses often are also the managers, the initial concern is with owners as investors in the business. Owners use financial statement data as a way to measure whether their money is working as hard in the business as it would be in an alternative investment. The data can also tell how well you or your managers have managed the firm's assets. Thus, the ratios that are of greatest interest to you as owner/investor are those that measure profitability relative to (1) your own investment in the firm and (2) the total amount invested in the firm from both your capital and borrowed funds.

1. ***How well is the company doing as an investment?*** - The *Return on Investment (ROI)* [Net Income ÷ Owners' Equity (Average)]

measures the profitability of the firm on owner-invested dollars. Net income is the after-tax return. The owners' equity (or capital) account is the investment. It is the amount you have contributed directly to the business and amounts that you have reinvested via undistributed profits.

ROI gives an indication of the past earning power of your investment and can be used to compare the company's performance in this regard to other companies in the industry. It should also be compared with other investment opportunities open to you. If your company typically generates a return of 10 percent and you can invest elsewhere at 15 percent, it doesn't make sense from a purely economic standpoint to keep your funds tied up in the company.

K-L Fashions' ROI for fiscal 2005 was about 12.7 percent [$147,430 ÷ $1,157,150]. Average owners' equity is used as the denominator to approximate the amount available for use in generating net income over the course of the entire year. Taken by itself, this figure is neither impressive not disturbing. The median "return on net worth" calculated by Dun and Bradstreet (D&B) for catalog and mail-order houses was 22.3 percent. The trend established over the last three years is more important. Comparing the 2005 return with the two preceding years, there is a sharp drop from 43.4 percent in 2003, to 28.2 percent in 2004, to 12.7 percent in 2005.

2.   ***How well has management employed the company's assets?*** - The *Return on Assets (ROA)* [Net Income ÷ Average Total Assets] measures the profitability of the firm on all invested dollars. That is, it measures how well the firm's assets have been employed in generating income. This measure is somewhat broader than the return on equity because it compares the returns on total capital. This includes the capital that you and the creditors have provided.

What constitutes a satisfactory ROA? It depends on the type of assets and their end use. Once again, since companies within a given industry tend to employ similar assets, your ROA should be measured against industry norms.
K-L Fashions' ROA for fiscal 2005 was 8.4 percent [$147,430 ÷ $1,761,660] compared with a median of 10 percent for the industry for the most recent period. Again, K-L Fashions falls short. We also see a declining ROA over a three-year period: 25 percent for 2003, 18.3 percent for 2004, and 8.4 percent for 2005.

(b)   Managers
Managers, too, are interested in measuring the operating performance in terms of profitability and return on invested capital. If they are not owners, managers must still satisfy the owners' expectations in this regard. As managers, they are interested in measures of operating efficiency, asset turnover, and liquidity or solvency. These will help them manage day-to-day activities and evaluate potential credit customers and key suppliers. Manager ratios serve as cash management tools by focusing on the management of inventory, receivables and payables. Accordingly, these ratios tend to focus on operating data reflected on the profit and loss statement and on the current sections of the balance sheet.

3.   *Are profits high enough, given the level of sales?* - In other words, how efficiently is management conducting operations? The *Net Profit Margin* [Net Income ÷ Sales (or Return on Sales) is a measure of the relative efficiency of the company's operations after deducting all expenses and income taxes. It measures the proportion of each sales dollar that results in net income.

The average for this ratio varies widely from industry to industry. To serve as an aid in management, the company's net profit margin should be compared with that of similar companies in the same industry, and with the company's past figures. The manager should monitor this ratio and investigate potential problems when the ratio begins to fall below the industry average or has shown continued deterioration during the most recent quarter or two. If both conditions exist, management is likely facing a problem that requires immediate attention. Incidentally, most bank loan officers use the return on sales ratio as a key indicator in making term loan decisions. A deteriorating ratio is often seen as an indication of impending business distress.

The fiscal 2005 net profit margin for K-L Fashions was 2.4 percent [147,430/6,039,750]. By comparison, the median return on sales for the industry, as reported by D&B, was 4.0 percent, meaning that another of the company's profitability measures is below the industry norm. Equally troubling is the downward trend in the net profit margin since 2003. In fiscal year 2004, the net profit margin was 5.3 percent, down from 7.1 percent for 2003. Over this period, profits declined 54.3 percent, despite a 32.5 percent increase in sales. If the company were maintaining operating efficiency, increases in sales would result in increases in profits (This scenario is generally an indication that some operating expenses are getting out of hand.) An examination of K-L Fashions' income statement suggests that selling, general and administrative expenses, which grew by 55 percent over the past two years, could be the cause of the decreased profitability. Because the financials for K-L Fashions only provide general categories, it is difficult to assess the cause of the increase in this expense category.

4. ***How well are the company's assets being employed to generate sales revenue?*** - The *Asset Turnover ratio* [Sales ÷ Average Total Assets] indicates the relative efficiency with which managers have used the firm's assets to generate output, and thus, it helps answer this question. Here again, what is acceptable or appropriate varies from industry to industry. Usually, however, a higher ratio is better. A very high turnover rate could signal an opportunity for expansion or the need for early replacement of assets. It could also mean that the company is in a high-volume, low-margin industry.

K-L Fashions' asset turnover ratio was 3.4 times [$6,039,750 ÷ $1,761,660] for fiscal 2005 and, despite a decrease from fiscal 2004, remains at a level comparable with fiscal year 2003. This means little by itself; but compared with the industry average of 3.1 times, we might conclude that sales performance is probably satisfactory for the amount of resources available.

Neither the profit margin nor the asset turnover by itself provides an adequate measure of operating efficiency or profitability. But multiplying the profit margin by the asset turnover ratio gives us the "Return on Assets" ratio or earnings power on total assets. This ratio is the same as the ROA computed for the owners but is presented in a form that managers often find more useful. It blends, in one number, all the major ingredients of profitability; yet it allows the manager to see how the individual components contribute. Thus, there are two basic ingredients to profitability; asset turnover and profit margin. An improvement in either -- without changing the other -- will increase the return on assets.

What can managers do to increase the returns on assets and owners' investments? The return on assets will increase by either an increase in the asset turnover or an increase in the profit margin. Three separate items are involved in the calculation: sales, net income, and assets. However, since net income is simply sales minus expenses, the three individual items subject to management control are sales, expenses and assets. Increasing sales, decreasing expenses, or decreasing assets, while holding the others constant, will improve the ROA and with it the ROI. Given K-L Fashions' most recent financial statement, it appears the most fruitful efforts would consist of controlling costs to increase both profits and the profit margin.

Notice that it doesn't require sophisticated analysis to come to this conclusion. This illustrates, however, one role of financial statement analysis: to highlight areas that need management attention. Once problem areas are highlighted, solutions can be obvious. This is why a common-sense approach of increasing sales and lowering expenses works to improve profitability.

5. ***Are receivables coming in too slowly?*** - The *Average Collection Period* [(Average A/R ÷ Annual Credit Sales) x 365] of receivables tells how many days, on average, customers' trade accounts (A/R) are outstanding. The average collection period is a measure of both liquidity and performance. As a measure of liquidity, it tells how long it takes to convert accounts receivable into cash. As a measure of performance, it indicates how well the company is managing the credit extended to customers.

Whether the average collection period is too high will depend on what kind of credit terms the company extends to its customers and how appropriate those terms are. If accounts are expected to be paid in 30 days, a 34-day average would be considered very good. Most customers tend to withhold payment for as long as the credit terms allow. This practice, along with some ever-present slow accounts, can cause the average collection period to exceed the stated limit by a week to 10 days and should not be a matter of concern. An average collection period of 48 days in this case, however, could be a danger signal. Customers, who are slow in paying their bills, may never pay at all.

As the balance sheet shows, K-L Fashions' accounts receivable are insignificant. The average collection period relating to all sales was .5 days [($7,785 ÷ $6,039,750) x 365] for 2005 and less than one-half day for each of the prior two year. This rapid turnover of receivables is understandable, because K-L Fashions' "credit sales" are largely bank credit card sales. Cash management in this area seems to be good in that no time is wasted in getting credit card invoices and personal checks credited to the company's account.

Because accounts receivables balances for K-L Fashions comprise a minor portion of the company's total assets, this ratio is not particularly useful as a cash management tool to its managers. And, as stated previously, a common-sense approach to financial statement analysis must be maintained. If, like K-L Fashions, your business has few receivables, then analysis of them would not be worthwhile. Another example is service industries that have no inventory. With no inventory, the next section of analysis is irrelevant.

6. ***Is too much cash tied up in inventories?*** - The *Inventory Turnover* [Cost of Goods Sold Expense ÷ Average Inventory] ratio is used to measure the speed with which inventories are being sold and is useful in managing inventory levels. How much inventory should the company keep on hand? The answer depends on making a delicate trade-off between anticipated near-term sales, the costs of ordering and holding inventory, the cost of stock-outs, etc. It also depends on the expected future availability of goods from the company's suppliers. In either case, excessive cash tied up in inventories reduces a company's solvency.

This ratio is vital for small-business managers who must make very effective use of the limited capital available to them. Just what is an appropriate turnover rate depends on the industry, the inventory itself, and general economic conditions. For example, the Brokaw Division of Wausau Papers (in Brokaw, Wisconsin) often has one to three years' worth of raw material inventory (logs) on hand. Because the road and weather conditions limit the time when wood can be received in Northern Wisconsin, Wausau Papers is forced to have a very slow inventory turnover rate for raw materials at that particular plant. However, finished goods (cut, colored paper) turn over every 28 days. If inventory turnover for the firm is consistently much slower than the average for the industry, then inventory stocks probably are either excessively high or contain a lot of obsolete items. Excessive inventories simply tie up funds that could be used to make needed debt payments or to expand operations. An extremely high turnover rate could be a sign of stock-outs -- not being able to fill a customer's order because the goods are not on hand. However, on the positive side, if neither stock-outs nor collections are a problem, then a high ratio can be good.

K-L Fashions' balance sheet also shows that, other than plant and equipment, more dollars have been invested in inventory than any other asset category. Given the type of firm, this is not unusual. However, the inventory turnover rate for the company is only 4.5 items per year [$3,573,070 ÷ $797,860], meaning that it takes an average of 81.5 days [365 ÷ 4.5] for the company to sell its inventory once it is purchased. This translates into about 81 days of inventory. Does this indicate too much inventory for the rate at which it is selling? On the surface it might seem excessive, considering that inventory balances should be at a low point after the Christmas sales rush. A look at similar companies, however, reveals that K-L Fashions' turnover is not much slower than the industry average of 5.1 times (or 72 days). Even with this level of inventory, management stated in its annual report that the company was able to fill only 82 percent of orders from goods on hand.

(c)   Short-Term Creditors

Short-term creditors, including managers who extend credit to trade customers, are interested in the solvency of borrowers or customers. As a result, they tend to focus on the current section of the balance sheet. The same calculations that a manager does on his/her own financial statements can also be done on a debtor's financial statements. The most widely used financial ratios used to answer questions of short-term solvency are the *current ratio* and *quick ratio.*

7.   ***Does this customer have sufficient cash or other liquid assets to cover its short-term obligations?*** - The *Current Ratio* [Current Assets ÷ Current Liabilities] is one of the most frequently used measures of solvency. It shows the relationship between current assets and current liabilities. Current liabilities are obligations that will come due in the next 12 months. Current assets are assets that are expected to be converted to cash in the same period. This ratio is widely used to provide one indication of whether a prospective customer or borrower is a good short-term credit risk. An old rule-of-thumb says that the current ratio should be at least 2.0 to provide an adequate margin of safety. Whether this ratio is high enough, however, depends on the type of company involved and, to some extent, on the time of year. (Airlines often have current ratios under 1.)

8.

What constitutes a good ratio also depends on the composition of the current assets relative to the due dates for the current obligations. If inventory makes up a significant portion of current assets and it is moving slowly, a higher-than-average ratio may hide potential liquidity problems. Thus, the quick ratio should also be evaluated.

The *Quick Ratio*= [Cash + Marketable Securities + A/R .
Current Liabilities] (or *acid test*)

This is a somewhat more accurate guide to short-term solvency. This ratio is the same as the current ratio except that it excludes inventory and prepaid expenses -- the least liquid of the current assets. It provides a more penetrating measure of solvency than does the current ratio. If receivables turn over rapidly, a quick ratio of 1.0 or a little higher is probably adequate. A grocery store will often have quick ratios of .25 to .50 and current ratios that exceed 2.

Suppose we are a supplier to K-L Fashions. K-L Fashions' current ratio at the end of fiscal year 2005 was 1.8 times ($1,078,240 ÷ $607,740), down from 2.3 times the previous year and below the industry median of 2.5 times. However, even if the latest current ratio were 2.3 or better, it alone would not provide us much comfort because inventory comprises so much of the company's current assets. K-L Fashions' latest quick ratio is .5 times ($284,730 ÷ $677,740) compared with an industry average of 1.0 times. This is a more stringent and valid test of liquidity in this case. If the ratio is at least 1.0 times (which means that liquid assets equal current liabilities), we can usually assume that the company has few short-term payment problems. At .5 times, however, we would want to look at other indicators of future cash flows. Any small company with these kinds of numbers may be required by creditors to provide a short-term projection of future cash receipts and disbursements.

8. ***How quickly does the prospective credit customer pay its bills?*** - Suppose that, on balance, we find the company's short-term solvency to be acceptable. Before agreeing to supply the company on a credit basis (or establishing credit terms for the company), we should try to determine how quickly the company normally pays its bills. The *Average Age of Payables* [(Average Payable ÷ Net Purchases) x 365] helps answer this question. That is, having determined that a company has the capacity to pay its short-term obligations as they come due (through the current or quick ratios), it is also important to evaluate its payment practice. In a manner similar to calculating the average collection period for accounts receivable, one can compute the average "age" of a company's payable, which is the average number of days it takes to pay its invoices. The age of the potential customer's payable will give a reasonable estimate of how soon a creditor can expect to be paid. This is particularly important for the small business that has just landed a major customer.

A large corporation is likely to use very effective (from its own standpoint) cash management procedures to ensure prompt payment from its customers while delaying payment to its suppliers as long as possible. Unless the small business is a critical supplier of its large corporate customer, that corporation may not accelerate its payment cycle to meet the supplier's cash flow needs. That's why it is critically important for the decision-making process of the small-business owner/manager to be able to estimate the potential customer's payment cycle.

To calculate the average age of payables for K-L Fashions, we need to estimate purchases because they are not reported directly in the statements. Cost of goods sold (which is on the income statement) equals beginning inventory, plus net purchases, minus ending inventory. Therefore, purchases equal the cost of goods sold ($3,573,070) minus beginning inventory $857,090) plus ending inventory ($738,630), or about $3,454,610. Using this calculation, we can calculate that the average age of K-L Fashions' payables is [($311,060 ÷ $3,454,610) x 365] = 32.9 days. If K-L Fashions were a potential customer, we should not expect it to pay our invoices much sooner than 33 days.

(d) Long-Term Creditors

Bankers and other long-term creditors want to be assured of receiving interest and principal when each becomes due. These creditors are particularly interested in the earning power and the present and future financial capacity of the borrower.

9. *As a potential or present long-term borrower, is the company's debt load excessive?* - If the company's debt load is too high -- it is highly leveraged -- it means that creditors of the firm have a disproportionately high share, and owners have a disproportionately low share, of the inherent risk of being in business. A simple measure of the "risk loan" is the *Debt-to-Equity (D/E)* [Total Debt ÷ Total Equity] ratio. This ratio relates the investment provided by creditors to that provided by owners. It indicates who the major risk-bearer in this business is. That is, if the D/E ratio is 10:1, it means that creditors have $10 invested in this business for every $1 that the owner has invested. Since the owner is making the decisions, the creditor in this case is in an extremely precarious position. The creditors in this case stand to lose 10 times as much as the company's owners. Therefore, the owner might be more willing to take more speculative risks.

Conversely, if the ratio is 1:10, it means that the owner has more to lose. The creditors for this type of company would feel safer knowing the owner has a bigger personal stake. From a creditor's standpoint, a lower D/E ratio is better. A long-term creditor tends to be skeptical of borrowers' good intentions or judgment when the company is highly leveraged or is seeking new funds that will cause it to become highly leveraged. Owners should use this ratio to view their companies as a long-term creditor would, and should seek to keep the debt-to-equity relationship within industry norms.

K-L Fashions' D/E is .6 ($685,740 ÷ $1,168,260), compared with a median D/E of .6 for the industry. This would normally indicate relative financial strength. However, we should note that those liabilities that do not need to be paid or settled in the near term, constitute only about 11 percent of total liabilities. Except for advance payments on orders the other 89 percent are short-term obligations. Consequently, this ratio is less important in this case than the short-term solvency measures -- even to the company's long-term creditors. This reinforces the concept that ratio analysis should be applied with common sense.

10. ***Are earnings and cash flow sufficient to cover interest payments and provide for some principal repayment?*** - The *Times Interest Earned (TIE)* [Income ÷ (Interest + Taxes) ÷ Interest Expense] ratio may be used to help answer this question. Note that this ratio uses income before interest and income taxes are subtracted because this is the amount of income available to cover interest. The larger the number, the easier it will be for the debtor company to suffer an earnings depression, and still make its interest payments. The TIE measures the bank's safety in terms of the likelihood that it will continue to receive periodic interest payments. The TIE does not, however, indicate how well *total* debt payments are covered.

The ***Cash Flow to Total Liabilities*** [Operating Cash Flow ÷ Total Liabilities] ratio is preferred by many bankers as a measure of earnings power relative to all debt. This debt coverage ratio depicts a company's debt repayment capability and is one of the more important indexes of long-term solvency. The cash flow figure in the numerator refers to net cash provided by operations as reported on the statement of cash flows in Figure 2. For small companies that don't prepare a cash flow statement, operating cash flow can be estimated by taking income before interest and taxes and adding back depreciation and other significant non-cash charges.

The industry average for this ratio is not likely to serve as a particularly useful benchmark. Bankers are more interested in the trend of the ratio. Increasing levels of debt without commensurate increases in cash generated by profitable operations is a sure sign of financial problems ahead. This could occur if the ROA is less than the borrowing rate.

K-L Fashions' earnings before interest and taxes is $259,610, compared with interest expense of $10,180. Thus, its interest coverage in terms of the times interest earned ratio is 25.5 times [$259,610 ÷ $10,180]. Although this ratio has declined substantially over the past three years, it has not declined as sharply as earnings because interest charges have declined. Furthermore, it is still quite large, indicating to creditors that interest payments are well covered.

K-L Fashions' cash flow statement shows that net cash provided by operations during fiscal year 2005 was $512,020, a substantial increase over both 2004 and 2003. Compared to the downward trend in net income, the cash flow from operations suggests the company has been reporting a large amount of non-cash expenses like depreciation and amortization. A likely cause in the increased non-cash charges is the large increases in land and buildings and in fixtures and equipment. Furthermore, it appears from the balance sheet that the expansion was financed by internally generated cash and without the assistance of long-term creditors. As these investments became productive, the company probably began depreciating them, resulting in the downward trend in net income. When these factors are considered, the decline in net profit margins does not look so serious.

The *cash flow to total liabilities ratio* [Operating Cash Flow ÷ Total Liabilities] is therefore $512,020 ÷ $685,740 = 74.7 percent. Standing alone, this ratio suggests that the company is conservatively capitalized and generates sufficient cash to cover its future obligations. The ratio is particularly healthy considering the fact that more than half of total debt is in the form of accounts payable, used to finance inventory and receivables.

4.0   SUMMARY

Compiling, analyzing, and understanding financial statements provides business owners one of the most important tools for reducing the considerable risk involved in starting and growing a business.   The comparison of financial ratios to industry standards is, perhaps, one of the best uses of financial information, as it allows the business owner to compare the performance of his or her business with other like businesses. In addition to providing information to owners critical for their own decision making, the accuracy of financial statements will impact the business' tax obligations and opportunities to obtain equity and/or debt financing. Careful record keeping leads to accurate financial statements, thereby reducing the business' tax burden. Business owners have the opportunity to compare their financial ratios with industry standards before applying for loans, thereby giving them the opportunity to correct any problems that could lead to the rejection of their business loan application or equity offering.

5.0   CONCLUSION

Regular preparation and analysis of financial statement information helps business managers and owners detect the problems that experts continue to see as the chief causes of business failure -- such as high, operating expenses, sluggish sales, poor cash management, excessive fixed assets, and inventory mismanagement. By comparing statements from different periods, you can more easily spot trends and make necessary management decisions and budget revisions before small problems become large ones.

6.0   PRACTICE ASSIGNMENT

Explain in detail how financial statements are interpreted and analyzed.

UNIT 2   BUSINESS MERGERS AND TAKEOVERS

CONTENTS

1.0   INTRODUCTION

In the world of business, mergers and acquisitions (take-over) constitute a powerful growth tool used by companies to achieve long-term growth and increased revenue or profitability. It is a tool used for expanding the operations of a company with a view to achieving growth.

In this unit, we shall examine mergers and acquisitions and its related matters.

2.0   OBJECTIVES

At the end of this unit, you should be able to:

*   explain merger and take-over (acquisition)
*   state the reasons for mergers and take-overs
*   state the legal and regulatory considerations for mergers and acquisition.

3.0   MAIN CONTENT

3.1   Mergers and Acquisitions

A merger connotes the combination of two companies into one larger company for some economic or other strategic reasons. It is defined as a transaction in which corporations of relatively equal size, combine. It is also seen as a transaction in which two or more corporations combine under state corporation law, with the result that all but one of the participating corporations lose its identity. Sherman and Hart describe a merger as – a combination of two or more companies in which the assets and liabilities of the selling firm(s) are absorbed by the buying firm. Although the buying firm may be a considerably different organization after the merger, it retains its originality.

The phrase "mergers" and "acquisitions" (abbreviated M&A) has been referred to as the aspect of corporate strategy, corporate finance and management dealing with the buying, selling and combining of different companies that can aid, finance, or help a growing company in a given industry, grow rapidly without having to create another business entity. Although they are often uttered in the same breath and used as though they were synonymous, the terms "merger" and "acquisition" mean slightly different things.

Mergers are vital tools used by companies for the purpose of expanding their business operations with objectives ranging from increasing their size, long term profitability or relevance within a particular market.

A merger is the fusion of two or more companies, as distinct from the *take-over* of one company by another. Mergers may be undertaken for various reasons, notably to improve the efficiency of two complementary companies by rationalizing output and taking advantage of economies of scale, and to fight off unwelcome takeover bids from other larger companies. The companies involved form one new company and their respective shareholders exchange their holding for shares in the new concern at an agreed rate. From a business perspective, a merger is simply the consolidation of two or more companies into one. Merger presupposes the existence of two independent things or estates, the greater of which would swallow up the lesser one by the process of absorption.

3.2   Forms of Business Combinations

1.   **Vertical Integration:** This is the combination of two firms which are in the same industry but at different stages in the producing and selling of products.
2.   **Horizontal Integration:** Where a firm takes over or merges with a company in the same industry and at the same level in that industry. It is a merger with a direct competitor.

3. Conglomerate Merger/Take-Over: This is a term used to describe merger between companies, in unrelated lines of business.

3.3 Business Mergers and Acquisitions

The year 1982 was a landmark year in the history of mergers and acquisitions in some countries. Prior to 1982 the concept of mergers and acquisitions had minimal actual significance. One of the very few major mergers that took place before that time was the amalgamation of three companies- Re Bendel Co Ltd, Bendel Intra-city Bus Service Ltd and Trans-Kalife Ltd- to form the Bendel Transport Service Ltd. This situation changed significantly after the Securities and Exchange Commission (SEC) began its operations in 1982, marking the beginning of regulated business combinations. The first merger attempt was in 1982 between United Italian Insurance Company Limited and United Life Insurance Company Limited, which was, however, not consummated. Between 1982 and 1988, the SEC supervised thirteen mergers- including the mergers of Lever Brothers Ltd and Lipton Ltd, SCOA Ltd and Automotive Components Ltd, John Holt Ltd and John Holt Investment Ltd- only two of which were unsuccessful.

The prospects of mergers and acquisitions in have continued to evolve since then. Different legislation have been passed to regulate business combinations, including the Companies and Allied Matters Act of 1990 and the *Investment and Securities Act* of 2007, as well as some sector- specific Acts, such as the Banking and other Financial Institutions Act of 1991, the Insurance Act of 2003 and the Electric Power Sector Reform Act of 2005. In 2002, there was a merger of two important petroleum companies; Agip Plc and Unipetrol Plc to form Oando Plc.

However, the most striking activities in mergers and acquisitions in Nigeria were undoubtedly the 2005 mergers that took place in the banking sector. These mergers were driven by the Central Bank of Nigeria's 2004 directive to all Nigerian banks to increase their shareholders' fund to a minimum of NGN25 Billion (twenty-five billion naira), from the previous minimum shareholders fund of NGN2 Billion (two billion naira). The deadline for this increase was December 31, 2005. Few Nigerian banks had this new minimum capital base, as a result, several mergers and acquisitions emerged, with only 25 out of 89 banks surviving the conditions and operating after 2005. Some of the banks formed as a result are Unity Bank Plc, Fin Bank Plc, Sterling Bank Plc, Fidelity Bank Plc, IBTC Chartered Bank Plc, Skye Bank Plc, Bank PHB and the United Bank for Africa.

SELF-ASSESSMENT EXERCISES (SAES) 1

1.   Define merger and acquisition.
2.   Trace the historical background of business mergers in Nigeria.

3.4   Reasons for Mergers & Acquisition

There are many reasons for companies wanting to acquire other companies. These reasons include the pursuit of a growth strategy, the defence of hostile action from another would-be acquirer, and financial opportunities. However, the commonest reason is that the merger will result in substantial trade advantage or greater profits than the combined profits of the two companies working separately. There is also the element of synergy.

More generally, motivation for takeovers and mergers may arise from the fact that cost of production would be less in a larger entity combined with enlarged operational capacity and reduction of duplications (the economies of scale). Mergers and acquisitions may enable a company acquire a competitor which poses substantial threat to it, or a company which supplies its raw materials or provides it with market outlets with the aim of assuring, improving these services, or ensuring that these companies are not taken-over by a competitor. Again, the motivation may be diversification of enterprises with a view to ensuring stability of earnings; and it may be to acquire the much-needed technology or managerial expertise of another company. Large combines have more obvious financial advantages than small companies. There is an enlarged capital base, loan capacity, accelerated growth and increased earnings.

There are reasons for going the route of mergers, which have been considered to primarily add to shareholder value. They are as follows: -

(a)   ***Economies of Scale:*** This refers to the fact that the combined company can often reduce duplicate units or operations, lowering the costs of the company relative to the same revenue stream, thus increasing profit.

Economies of scale that would result in a reduction in costs and utilization of the synergies between the two merging entities to streamline operation was also cited as one of the reasons for the merger between Dangote Cement Plc and Benue Cement Plc.

(b)   ***Increased Revenues/ Increased Market Share:*** This motive assumes that the company will be absorbing a major competitor and thus increase its power (by capturing increased market share) to set prices.

(c) **Cross Selling**: For example, a bank buying a stock broker could then sell its banking products to the stock broker's customers, while the broker can sign up the bank's customers for brokerage accounts, or a manufacturer can acquire and sell complementary products.

(d) **Synergy**: Better use of complementary resources. Excluding any synergies resulting from the merger, the total post-merger value of the two firms is equal to the pre-merger value. However, the post-merger value of each individual firm likely will be different from the pre-merger value because the exchange ratio of the shares probably will not exactly reflect the firms' values with respect to one another. The exchange ratio is often skewed because the target firm's shareholders are paid a premium for their shares.

Synergy takes the form of revenue enhancement and cost savings. When two companies in the same industry merge, such as two banks, combined revenue tends to decline to the extent that the businesses overlap in the same market and some customers become alienated. For the merger to benefit shareholders there should be cost saving opportunities to offset the revenue decline; the synergies resulting from the merger must be more than the initial lost value.

(e) **Taxes**: A profitable company can buy a loss maker to use the target's loss as their advantage by reducing their tax liability. In the United States and many other countries, rules are in place to limit the ability of profitable companies to "shop" for loss-making companies, limiting the tax motive of an acquiring company.

(f) **Geographical or other diversification**: This is designed to smooth the earnings results of a company, which over a long term, smoothens the share price of a company, giving conservative investors more confidence in investing in the company. However, this does not always deliver value to shareholders.

(g) **Resource Transfer**: Resources are unevenly distributed across firms and the interaction of target and acquiring firm resources can create value through either overcoming information asymmetry or by combining scarce resources.

(h) **Increased market share which can increase market power**: In an oligopoly, increased market share generally allows companies to raise prices. Note that while this may be in the shareholders' interest, it often raises antitrust concerns, and may not be in the public interest.

The reasons for a merger could also be appreciated from the perspective of the seller. The reasons include –

(a)   The seller could be approaching retirement or getting ready for an exit out of the business.

(b)   The need for competent management or managers that could lead the business to the next level i.e. sustain it.

(d)   The business could require substantial investment in new technology and business processes to enhance its competiveness.

(e)   The need for access to the target's resources coupled with the need for liquid assets to augment working capital, and meet critical obligations of the company.

The reasons for merging could also be appreciated from the buyer's perspective. The reasons would include –

(a)   The need to enhance revenues, and reduce the operation costs relative to the revenues. In essence to increase the earnings per share (EPS). Mergers in which the acquiring company's earnings per share (EPS) increases is known as "accretive mergers". An alternative way of calculating this is if a company with a high price to earnings ratio (P/E) acquires one with a low P/E. The corollary of accretive mergers is "dilutive mergers", whereby a company's EPS decreases. The company will be one with a low P/E acquiring one with a high P/E.

(b)   Backward or vertical integration (vertical or horizontal operational synergies) or economies of scale.

(c)   The need to acquire new technologies, business processes, production capacity and management capabilities.

(d)   Strengthening management capabilities.

(e)   Change in the overall direction of the business.

3.5   Understanding commonly used M&A vocabulary

It is expected that you that you should know the following terms:

i.   Statutory Merger: Combination of two corporations in which only one corporation survives in accordance with the statutes of the state in which the surviving firm is incorporated.

ii.   Subsidiary Merger: A merger of two companies resulting in the target company becoming a subsidiary of the parent.

iii.   Consolidation: Two or more companies join to form a new company.

iv.   Acquisition: Purchase of an entire company or a controlling interest in a company.

v.   Divestiture: The sale of all or substantially all of a company or product line to another party for cash or securities.

vi.   LBO: The purchase of a company financed primarily by debt. The term is more often applied to a firm going private financed primarily by debt.

vii. Management buyout: A leveraged buyout in which the managers of the firm to be taken private are also equity investors.

viii. Holding company: A single company with investments in a number of other, often diverse, operating companies.

ix.   Acquirer: A firm attempting to merge or acquire another company

x.   Target: The firm being solicited by the acquiring firm.

xi.   Horizontal merger: Occurs when two firms in the same industry combine.

xii. Vertical merger: Mergers in which the two firms are in different stages of the value chain.

xiii. Conglomerate mergers: Mergers between companies in largely unrelated industries.

xiv. Friendly takeovers: The target's management and board are receptive to being acquired and recommend that the shareholders approve the transaction.

xv.   Hostile takeover: Occurs when the initial offer was unsolicited by the target, the target was not seeking a merger at the time it was approached, and the target's management contested the offer

xvi. Takeover premium: The excess of the purchase price over the target's current share price.

3.6   Legal and Regulatory Considerations

When one company decides to acquire another company, a series of negotiations will take place between the two companies. The acquiring company will have a well-developed negotiating strategy and plan in place. If the Target Company believes a merger is possible, the two companies will enter into a "Letter of Intent."

The Letter of Intent outlines the terms for future negotiations and commits the Target Company to giving serious consideration to the merger. A Letter of Intent also gives the acquiring company the green light to move into Phase II Due Diligence. The Letter of Intent attempts to answer several issues concerning the proposed merger:

1.   How will the acquisition price be determined?

2.   What exactly are we acquiring? Is it physical assets, is it a controlling interest in the target, is it intellectual capital, etc.?

3.   How will the merger transaction be designed? Will it be an outright purchase of assets? Will it be an exchange of stock?

4.   What is the form of payment? Will the acquiring company issue stock, pay cash, issue notes, or use a combination of stock, cash, and/or notes?

5.   Will the acquiring company setup an escrow account and deposit part of the purchase price? Will the escrow account cover unrecorded liabilities discovered from due diligence?

6.   What is the estimated time frame for the merger? What law firms will be responsible for creating the M & A Agreement?

7.   What is the scope of due diligence? What records will be made available for completing due diligence?

8.   How much time will the Target Company allow for negotiations? The Letter of Intent will usually prohibit the Target Company from "shopping itself" during negotiations.

9.   How much compensation (referred to as bust up fees) will the acquiring company be entitled to in the event that the target is acquired by another company? Once news of the proposed merger leaks out, the Target Company is "in play" and other companies may make a bid to acquire the Target Company.

10.   Will there be any operating restrictions imposed on either company during negotiations? For example, the two companies may want to postpone hiring new personnel, investing in new facilities, issuing new stock, etc. until the merger has been finalized.

11.   If the two companies are governed by two states or countries, which one will govern the merger transaction?
      Will there be any adjustment to the final purchase price due to anticipated losses or events prior to the closing of the merger?

4.0   CONCLUSION

In this unit, we examined mergers and acquisition, the various forms of business integration as well as the historical background of mergers and acquisitions. The reasons for mergers and take-overs and the legal considerations were treated.

5.0   SUMMARY

Mergers and acquisitions are among the most difficult of business transactions. There is no shortage of stress. There are numerous reasons why companies decide to merge. Some studies indicate that companies merge for improving efficiencies and lowering costs. Other studies show that companies merge to increase market share and gain a competitive advantage. The ultimate goal behind a merger and acquisition is to generate synergy values. Good strategic planning is the key to understanding if synergy values do in fact exist. A well-researched and realistic plan will dramatically improve the chances of realizing synergy values.

SELF-ASSESSMENT EXERCISES

i.   Define letter of intent.
ii.   What questions are answered by letter of intent?

6.0   TUTOR-MARKED ASSIGNMENT

What are the reasons for mergers and take-overs?

MODULE 4

UNIT 1   DIVIDEND POLICY

CONTENTS

1.0   Introduction
2.0   Objectives
3.0   Main Content
    3.1   Dividend Policy
    3.2   Factors influencing dividend policy
    3.3   Dividends as a signal to investors
    3.4   Theories of Dividend Policy
    3.5   Alternative to Cash Dividends
4.0   Conclusion
5.0   Summary
6.0   Tutor-Marked Assignment

1.0   INTRODUCTION

Shareholders normally have power to vote to reduce the size of the dividend at the AGM, but not the power to increase the dividend. This, therefore, requires understanding by every shareholder as well other stakeholders. In light of the above, in this unit, we shall examine dividend policy.

2.0   OBJECTIVES

At the end of this unit, you should be able to:

- define dividend policy
- explain the impact that the issue of dividends may have on a company's share price
- explain the theory of dividend irrelevance
- discuss the influence of shareholder expectations on the dividend decision
- discuss the influence of liquidity constraints on the dividend decision
- define and distinguish between bonus issues and scrip dividends
- discuss the implications of share repurchase.

3.0   MAIN CONTENT

3.1   Dividend Policy

Shareholders normally have **power to vote to reduce the size** of the dividend at the AGM, but **not the power to increase the dividend**. The directors of the company are therefore in a strong position, with regard to shareholders, when it comes to determining dividend policy. For practical purposes, shareholders will usually be obliged to accept the dividend policy that has been decided on by the directors, or otherwise to sell their shares.

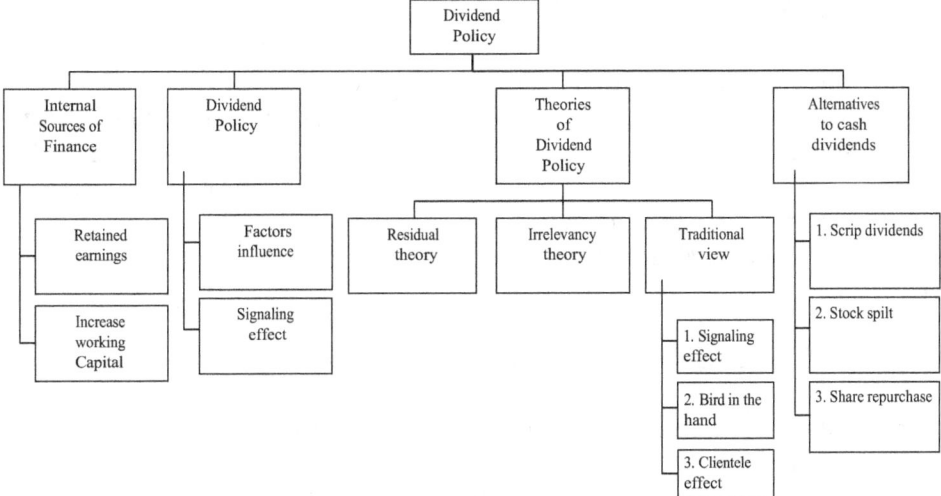

Fig. 1. Dividend Policy
The above figure illustrates the structure of dividend policy.

3.2   Factors Influencing Dividend Policy

When deciding upon the dividends to pay out to shareholders, one of the main considerations of the directors will be the amount of earnings they wish to retain to meet **financing needs**. As well as future financing requirements, the decision on how much of a company's profit should be retained, and how much paid out to shareholders, will be influenced by:

(a)   The **need to remain profitable** – dividends are paid out of profits, and an unprofitable company cannot for ever go on paying dividends out of retained profits made in the past.

(b)   The **law on distributable profits** – a Company Act may make companies bound to pay dividends solely out of **accumulated net realized profits** as in the UK.

(c)   The government which may impose **direct restrictions** on the amount of dividends companies can pay. For example, in the UK in the 1960's as part of a prices and income policy.

(d)   Any **dividend restraints** that might be imposed by **loan agreements**.

(e)   The **effect of inflation**, and the need to retain some profit within the business just to maintain its operating capability unchanged.

(f)   The company's **gearing level** – if the company wants extra finance, the sources of funds used should strike a balance between equity and debt finance.

(g)   The company's **liquidity position** – dividends are a cash payment, and a company must have enough cash to pay the dividends it declares.

(h)   The need to **repay debt** in the near future.

(i)   The **ease** with which the company could raise **extra finance** from sources other than retained earnings – small companies which find it hard to raise finance might have to rely more heavily on retained earnings than large companies.

(i) The **signaling effect** of dividends to shareholders and the financial markets in general.

SELF-ASSESSMENT EXERCISE

Discuss the factors to be considered in formulating the dividend policy of a stock exchange listed company.

3.3   Dividends as a signal to investors

Although the market would like to value shares on the basis of underlying cash flows on the company's projects, such information is **not readily available to investors** But the directors do have this information. The dividend declared can be interpreted as a **signal** from directors to shareholders about the **strength of underlying project cash flows**.

Investors usually expect a **consistent dividend policy** from the company, with stable dividends each year or, even better, **steady dividend growth**. A large rise or fall in dividends in any year can have a marked effect on the company's share price.

Stable dividends or steady dividend growth are usually needed for share price stability. A **cut in dividends** may be treated by investors as signaling that the **future prospects of the company are weak**.

The **signaling effect** of a company's dividend policy may also be used by management of a company which faces a possible **takeover**. The **dividend level** might be **increased as a defence against the takeover** – investors may take the **increased dividend as a signal of improved future prospects**, thus driving the share price higher and making the company more expensive for a potential bidder to take over.

3.4   Theories of Dividend Policy

3.4.1 Residual theory

A residual theory of dividend policy can be summarized as follows.

(a)   If a company can identify projects with positive NPVs, it should invest in them

(b)   Only when these investment opportunities are exhausted should dividends be paid.

3.4.2 Irrelevancy theory

Miller and Modigliani showed that, in a perfect capital market, the value of a company depended on its investment decision alone, and not on its dividend or financing decisions.

In such a market, a change in dividend policy would not affect its share price or its market capitalization. They showed that the value of a company was maximized if it invested in all projects with a positive net present value (its optimal investment schedule).

The company could pay any level of dividend and if it had insufficient finance, make up the shortfall by issuing new equity.
Since investors had perfect information, they were indifferent between dividends and capital gains.

Shareholders who were unhappy with the level of dividend declared by a company could gain a 'home-made dividend' by selling some of their shares. This was possible since there are no transaction costs in a perfect capital market.

3.4.3 Traditional view

The traditional view of dividend policy, implicit in our earlier discussion, is to focus on the effects on share price. The price of a share depends upon the mix of dividends, given shareholders' required rate of return, and growth.

(a) **Signaling effect**

   Dividend signaling – as mentioned in 2.3 above, an increase in dividends would signal greater confidence in the future by managers and would lead investors to increase their estimate of future earnings and cause a rise in the share price.

   This argument implies that dividend policy is relevant. Firms should attempt to adopt a stable (and rising) dividend payout to maintain investors' confidence.

(b) **Preference for current income (bird in the hand)**

   Many investors require cash dividends to finance current consumption. This does not only apply to individual investors needing cash to live on but also to institutional investors, e.g. pension funds and insurance companies, who require regular cash inflows to meet day-to-day outgoings such as pension payments and insurance claims. This implies that many shareholders will prefer companies who pay regular cash dividends and will therefore value the shares of such a company more highly.

(c) **Clientele effect**

   In many situations, income in the form of **dividends is taxed** in a different way from income in the form of capital gains. This distortion in the personal tax system can have an **impact on investors' preferences**.

   From the corporate point of view this further complicates the dividend decision as different groups of shareholders are likely to prefer different payout patterns.

   One suggestion is that companies are likely to attract a clientele of investors who favor their dividend policy. For example, higher rate tax payers may prefer capital gains to dividend income as they can choose the timing of the gain to minimize the tax burden. In this case companies should be very cautious in making significant changes to dividend policy as it could upset their investor

   Research in the US tends to confirm this **clientele effect** with high dividend payout firms attracting low income tax bracket investors and low dividend payout firms attracting high income tax bracket investors.

(d)   Information asymmetry
Real world capital markets are not perfect, **perfect information** is therefore **not available**, it is possible for information asymmetry to exist between shareholders and the managers of a company.

Dividend announcements may **give new information to shareholders** and as a result, in a semi-strong form efficient market, **share prices may change**.

3.5   Alternative to Cash Dividends

3.5.1 Scrip dividends

A scrip dividend is a **dividend paid by the issue of additional company shares**, rather than by cash.

When the directors of a company would prefer to retain funds within the business but consider that they must at least a certain amount of dividend, they might offer equity shareholders the choice of a cash dividend or a scrip dividend.

Advantages of scrip dividends
(a)   They can **preserve** a company's **cash position** if a substantial number of shareholders take up the share option.
(b)   Investors may be able to obtain **tax advantages** if dividends are in the term of shares.
(c)   Investors looking to **expand their holding** can do so **without incurring the transaction costs** of buying more shares.
(d)   A small scrip dividend issue will **not dilute the share price significantly**. If however cash is not offered as an alternative, empirical evidence suggests that the share price will tend to fall.
(e)   A share issue will **decrease** the company's **gearing**, and may therefore **enhance its borrowing capacity**.
Disadvantage of scrip dividends:
(a)   If affects in future years, because the number of shares in issue has increased, the **total cash dividend will increase**, assuming the dividend per share is maintained or increased.

3.5.2 Stock split

A stock split occurs where, for example, each ordinary share of $1 each is spilt into two shares of 50cent each, thus creating cheaper shares with greater marketability. There is possibly an added psychological advantage, in that investors may expect a company which splits its shares in this way to be planning for substantial earnings growth and dividend growth in the future. As a consequence, the **market price of shares may benefit**. For example, if one existing share of $1 has a market value of $6, and is then split into two shares of 50cent each, the market value of the new shares might settle at,say, $3.10 instead of the expected $3, in anticipation of strong future growth in earnings and dividends.

The **difference between a stock split and a scrip issue** is that a **scrip issue coverts equity reserves into share capital**, whereas a stock split leaves reserves unaffected.

3.5.3 Share repurchase

Purchase by a company of its own shares can take place for various reasons and must be in accordance with any requirements of legislation.

For a smaller company with few shareholders, the reason for buying back the company's own shares may be that there is no immediate willing purchaser at a time when a shareholder wishes to sell shares. For a public company, share repurchase could provide a way of withdrawing from the share market and **going private**.

Benefits of a share repurchase scheme
(a)   Finding a **use of surplus cash**, which may be a **dead asset**.
(b)   **Increase in earnings per share** through a reduction in the number of shares in issue. This should lead to a higher share price than would otherwise be the case, and the company should be able to increase dividend payments on the remaining shares in issue.
(c)   **Increase in gearing.** Repurchase of a company's own shares allows debt to be substituted for equity, so raising gearing. This will be of interest to a company wanting to increase its gearing without increasing its total long-term funding.
(d)   **Readjustment of the company's equity base** to more appropriate levels, for a company whose business is in decline.
(e)   Possibly **preventing a takeover** or enabling a quoted company to withdraw from the stock market.
         Drawbacks of a share repurchase scheme
         (a)   It can be **hard to arrive at a price** that will be fair both to the vendors and to any shareholders who are not selling shares to the company.

(b) A repurchase of shares could be seen as an **admission** that the company **cannot make better use of the funds** than the shareholders.

(c) Some shareholders may suffer from being **taxed on a capital gain** following the purchase of their shares rather than receiving dividend income.

4.0 CONCLUSION

This unit examined dividend policy as well as related concepts.

5.0 SUMMARY

Shareholders normally have power to vote to reduce the size of the dividend at the AGM, but not the power to increase the dividend. This, therefore, requires understanding by every shareholder as well other stakeholders. In light of the above, in this unit, we shall examine dividend policy.

When deciding upon the dividends to pay out to shareholders, one of the main considerations of the directors will be the amount of earnings they wish to retain to meet financing needs.

SELF-ASSESSMENT EXERCISE

i.   Discuss the factors to be considered in formulating the dividend policy of a stock exchange listed company.
ii.   Discuss the theories of dividend policy.
iii. Explain the nature of a scrip (share) dividend and discuss the advantages and disadvantages to a company of using scrip dividends to reward shareholders.

6.0 TUTOR-MARKED ASSIGNMENT

AB and YZ both operate department stores in Nigeria. They operate in similar markets and are generally considered to be direct competitors. Both companies have had similar earnings records over the past ten years and have similar capital structures. The earnings and dividend record of the two companies over the past six years is as follows:

Year to 31 March	AB EPS Naira	DPS Naira	Average share price	YZ EPS Naira	DPS Naira	Average share price
2006	230	60	2,100	240	96	2,200
2007	150	60	1,500	160	64	1,700
2008	100	60	1,000	90	36	1,400
2009	– 125	60	800	– 100	0	908
2010	100	60	1,000	90	36	1,250
2011	150	60	1,400	145	58	1,700

Note: EPS = Earnings per share and DPS = Dividends per share
AB has had 25 million shares in issue for the past six years. YZ currently has 25 million shares in issue. At the beginning of 2010 had a 1 for 4 rights issue. The EPS and DPS have been adjusted in the above table.

The Chairman of AB is concerned that the share price of YZ is higher than his company, despite the fact that AB has recently earned more per share than YZ and frequently during the past six years has paid a higher dividend.

Required:
(a)   Discuss:
   (i)   the apparent dividend policy followed by each company over the past six years and comment on the possible relationship of these policies to the company's market values and current share prices; and
   (ii)   Whether there is an optimal dividend policy for AB that might increase shareholder value.

(12 marks)
(b)   Forecast earnings for AB for the year to 31 March 2012 are N40 million. At present, it has excess cash of N2.5 million and is considering a share repurchase in addition to maintaining last year's dividend. The Chairman thinks this will have a number of benefits for the company, including a positive effect on the share price.
Advise the Chairman of AB of

   (i)   How a share repurchases may be arranged;
   (ii)   The main reasons for a share repurchase;
   (iii)   The potential problems of such an action, compared with a one-off extra dividend payment, and any possible effect on the share price of AB.

(13 marks)

Note: A report format is not required for this question.

(Total 25 marks)

UNIT 2   VALUATION OF SHARES

CONTENTS

1.0   INTRODUCTION

Valuation of shares is important in so many areas as shall be seen in subsequent sub-units of this unit. However, this topic does not only require the understanding of one or two accounting techniques, but also an in-depth appreciation of many commercial and financial matters.
This unit therefore examines shares valuation and the various methods of valuing shares.

2.0   OBJECTIVES

At the end of this unit, you should be able to:

- explain valuation of shares
- state the various methods of valuing shares.

3.0   MAIN CONTENT

3.1   Valuation of Share

For anyone involved in the field of corporate finance, understanding the mechanisms of company valuation is an indispensable requisite. This is not only because of the importance of valuation in acquisitions and mergers but also because the process of valuing the company and its business units helps identify sources of economic value creation and destruction within the company.

In spite of the given quoted prices of a company on the Stock Exchange, there is need to devise techniques for estimating the value of its share. However, a share valuation is also necessary for both listed and unlisted companies because of certain circumstances.

The circumstances are as follows:

(a)   For quoted companies, when there is a take-over bid and the offer price is an estimated "fair value" in excess of the current market price of the shares;

(b)   For unquoted companies, when;
   i)   The company wishes to "go public" and must fix an issue price for its share;
   ii)   There is a scheme of merger, and a value of shares for each company involved in the merger must be assessed;
   iii)   Shares are sold;
   iv)   Shares need to be valued for the purpose of taxation;
   v)   Shares are pledged as collateral as loan.

(c)   For subsidiary companies, when the group's holding company is negotiating the sale of the subsidiary to a management buy-out team or to an external buyer

In general terms, **a valuation may be used for a wide range of purposes**:

1.   *In company buying and selling operations:*
      For the buyer, the valuation will tell him the highest price he should pay.
      i.   For the seller, the valuation will tell him the lowest price at which he should be prepared to sell.

2.   *Valuations of listed companies:*
      i.   The valuation is used to compare the value obtained with the share's price on the stock market and to decide whether to sell, buy or hold the shares.
      ii.   The valuation of several companies is used to decide the securities that the portfolio should concentrate on: those that seem to it to be undervalued by the market.
      iii.   The valuation of several companies is also used to make comparisons between companies. For example, if an investor thinks that the future course of ABC's share price will be better than that of XYZ, he may buy ABC shares and short-

sell XYZ shares. With this position, he will gain provided that ABC's share price does better (rises more or falls less) than that of XYZ.

3.   ***Public offerings:***
   i.   The valuation is used to justify the price at which the shares are offered to the public.

4.   ***Inheritances and wills:***
   i.   The valuation is used to compare the shares' value with that of the other assets.

5.   ***Compensation schemes based on value creation:***
   i.   The valuation of a company or business unit is fundamental for quantifying the value creation attributable to the executives being assessed.

6.   ***Identification of value drivers:***
   i.   The valuation of a company or business unit is fundamental for identifying and stratifying the main value drivers

7.   ***Strategic decisions on the company's continued existence:***
   i.   The valuation of a company or business unit is a prior step in the decision to continue in the business, sell, merge, milk, grow or buy other companies.

8.   ***Strategic planning:***
   ii.   The valuation of the company and the different business units is fundamental for deciding what products/business lines/countries/customers … to maintain grow or abandon.
   iii.   The valuation provides a means for measuring the impact of the company's possible policies and strategies on value creation and destruction.

3.2   Value and price: What purpose does a valuation serve?

Generally speaking, a company's value is different for different buyers and it may also be different for the buyer and the seller.

Value should not be confused with price, which is the quantity agreed between the seller and the buyer in the sale of a company. This difference in a specific company's value may be due to a multitude of reasons.

For example, a large and technologically highly advanced foreign company wishes to buy a well-known national company in order to gain entry into the local market, using the reputation of the local brand. In this case, the foreign buyer will only value the brand but not the plant, machinery, etc. as it has more advanced assets of its own. However, the seller will give a very high value to its material resources, as they are able to continue producing.

From the buyer's viewpoint, the basic aim is to determine the maximum value it should be prepared to pay for what the company it wishes to buy is able to contribute. From the seller's viewpoint, the aim is to ascertain what should be the minimum value at which it should accept the operation.

These are the two figures that face each other across the table in a negotiation until a price is finally agreed on, which is usually somewhere between the two extremes. There is also the middle position that considers both the buyer's and seller's viewpoints and is represented by the figure of the neutral arbitrator. Arbitration is often necessary in litigation, for example, when dividing estates between heirs or deciding divorce settlements.

A company may also have different values for different buyers due to economies of scale, economies of scope, or different perceptions about the industry and the company.

3.3 Key factors affecting value: growth, return, risk and interest rates

The equity's value depends on expected future flows and the required return to equity. In turn, the growth of future flows depends on the return on investments and the company's growth. However, the required return to equity depends on a variable over which the company has no control, the risk-free interest rate, and on the equity's risk which, in turn, we can divide into operating risk and financial risk.

The equity's value depends on three primary factors (*value drivers*): expectations of future flows; required return to equity; and communication with the market.

The communication with the market factor not only refers to communication and transparency with the markets in the strict sense but also to communication with: analysts, rating companies, regulatory agencies, board of directors, employees, customers, distribution channels, partner companies, suppliers, financial institutions, and shareholders. The three primary factors can be subdivided in turn into return on the investment, company growth, risk-free interest rate, market risk premium, operating risk and financial risk. However, these factors are still very general. It is very important that a company identify the fundamental parameters that have most influence on the value of its shares and on value creation. Obviously, each factor's importance will vary for the different business units.

3.4   Methods of Shares Valuation

The most common methods of valuing shares are:

1.   The earnings method (P/E Ratio)
2.   The Accounting Rate of Return (ARR)
3.   The net assets
4.   CAPM method
5.   Super Profit method
6.   The Dividend yield
7.   DCF-based valuation
8.   Share Prices

Please note that each method gives a different share valuation. And in most cases, a method is not used in isolation.

(a)   The Price/Earnings Ratio (Earnings Method)

The P/E ratio method is widely used in practice.
This method relies on finding listed companies in similar businesses to the company being valued (the target company), and then looking at the relationship they show between share price and earnings. Using that relationship as a model, the share price of the target company can be estimated.

The P/E ratio is the price per share divided by the earnings per share and shows how many years' worth of earnings are paid for in the share price.

P/E Ratio = $\dfrac{\text{Market Value}}{\text{EPS}}$

Where:
Market Value= EPS X P/E Ratio

General guidelines for a P/E ratio-based valuation
When a company is thinking of acquiring an unquoted company in a take-over, the final offer price will be agreed by negotiation, but a list of some of the factors affecting the valuer's choice of P/E ratio is given below.

i.   General economic and financial conditions
ii.   The type of industry and the prospects of that industry
iii.   The size of the undertaking and its status within its industry.
iv.   The reliability of profit estimates and the past profit record.
v.   Asset backing and liquidity

vi.   The extent to which the business is dependent on the technical skills of one or more individuals.

Illustration 1

Ammar Limited wishes to make a take-over bid for the shares of an unquoted company, Yaasir Limited over the past five years have been as follows.

2001	$500,000
2002	$720,000
2003	$680,000
2004	$710,000
2005	$750,000

The average P/E ratio of quoted companies in the industry in which Yaasir Limited operates is 10. Quoted companies which are similar in many respects to Ammar Limited are:

i.   Sumayyah Plc., which has a P/E ratio of 15, but is a company with very good growth prospects;
ii.   Fidel Plc., had a poor profit record for several years, and has a P/E ratio of 7;
iii.   What would be a suitable range of valuations for the shares of Yaasir Limited?

Solution

i.   Earnings: Average earnings over the last five years have been $672,000 and over the last four years $715,000. There might appear to be some growth prospects, but estimates of future earnings are uncertain. A low estimate of earnings in 2006 would be, perhaps, $715,000.
ii.   A high estimate of earnings might be $750,000 or more. This solution will use the most recent earnings figure of $750,000 as the high estimate.
iii.   P/E ratio: A P/E ratio of 15 (Sumayyah Plc.) would be much too high for Yaasir Ltd, because the growth of Yaasir Ltd earnings is not certain and Yaasir Ltd is an unquoted company.

On the other hand, Yaasir Ltd's expectations of earnings are probably better than those of Fidel Plc. A suitable P/E ratio might be based on the industry's average, 10; but since Yaasir Ltd is an unquoted company and therefore riskier, a lower P/E ratio might be more appropriate. Perhaps 60% to 70% of 10 which is 6 or 7; or conceivably even as low as 50% of 10, that is 5.

The valuation of Yaasir Ltd's shares might therefore range between;
High P/E ratio and high earnings: 7 X $750,000 = $5,250,000
Low P/E ratio and low earnings: 5 X $715,000 = $3,575,000

(b)   The Accounting rate of Return Method

This method considers the ARR which will be required from the company whose shares are to be valued. It is distinct from the P/E ratio method. The ARR method involves using a predetermined notion of the rate of return an investor would expect on a particular type of investment and then having decided on the earnings of the company, to calculate capital sum that would result in such a rate of return.

Formula:

Value = $\dfrac{\text{Estimated future profits}}{\text{Return on capital employed}}$

Illustration 2

Paul Ltd is considering acquiring Peter Ltd. At present, Peter Ltd is earning on average, $48,000,000 after tax. The directors of Paul Ltd feel that after reorganization, this figure could increase to $60,000,000. All the companies in Paul's group are expected to yield a post-tax accounting return of 15% on capital employed. What should Peter Ltd be valued at?

Solution

Valuation = $\dfrac{\$60,000,000}{15\%}$ =$400,000,000

(c)   Net Asset Basis

The method considers all tangible assets less all intangible assets. This means that we should consider only the tangible assets but intangible assets such as goodwill, patents, trademarks, preliminary expenses should not be assigned with any value. This must be calculated whether requested or not. The difficulty in asset valuation method is not in the arithmetic involved, but in the process of establishing the asset value to use.

The net asset method of valuation should be used:

(a)   When the company is on the verge of liquidation
(b)   When unquoted shares are offered as collateral for loans.
(c)   As a measure of comparison in a scheme of merger.
(d)   As a measure of the security in a share value.
(d)   Dividend Yield Method

This method is suitable for the valuation of small shareholdings in unquoted companies. It is based on the principle that the value of a share is the present value of future dividend payments, discounted at a suitable (marginal) rate of shareholder's time preference.

There are two approaches under this technique using net and gross dividends.

(a)   Dividend with growth
(b)   Dividend with growth

Dividend without growth:
Recall that $K_e = \dfrac{d}{MV}$

$MV = \dfrac{d}{K_e\ (r)}$

Net dividend = Dividend (net)/Required rate of return
Gross dividend = Dividend (gross)/Required rate of return
Dividend with growth:
Growth model: $MV = \dfrac{d_0\ (1+g)}{r - g}$

(e)   Share Prices

These are prices quoted on the stock Exchange. Users are to use the quoted prices to multiply the number of shares under consideration.

4.0   CONCLUSION

This unit examined the valuation of shares of companies and its purposes. The key factors affecting values as well as the various methods of share valuation were also considered.

5.0   SUMMARY

In making a bid for another company, it is important for the buyer to create a range of values within which a buyer would be prepared to negotiate. When deciding to float or sell the company again the seller must value the shares and create a range of values within which to negotiate. Hence the need for valuation of shares.

6.0   TUTOR-MARKED ASSIGNMENT

What is share valuation? Discuss the various methods of share valuation.

UNIT 3   ASSET MANAGEMENT

CONTENTS

1.0   Introduction
2.0   Objectives
3.0   Main Content
    3.1 Asset Management
    3.2 What Asset Management is and isn't
4.0   Conclusion
5.0   Summary
6.0   Tutor-Marked Assignment

1.0   INTRODUCTION

Asset Management is increasingly well understood by the business community as a strategic and business led discipline, where the value of assets is their contribution to achieving explicit business objectives. The understanding of asset management and its component is therefore crucial. In this unit, you shall learnt what surrounds the foregoing.

2.0   OBJECTIVES

At the end of this unit, you should be able to:

- define asset management
- state what constitute asset management and what does not.
- discuss the functions of an asset manager.
- state the importance of asset management

3.0   MAIN CONTENT

3.1   Asset Management

Asset has been defined as "any item of economic value owned by an individual or corporation". And Asset Management is increasingly well understood by the business community as a strategic and business led discipline, where the value of assets is their contribution to achieving explicit business objectives.

A good 'asset management' decision might be to purchase *an expensive, high specification* stainless steel piping system within an industrial process. Whilst the initial cost is higher, the maintenance costs may be lower and the expected life 3 times longer, the risk of disruptive failure may be lower and therefore the risk to the organization from a performance, health & safety and environmental perspective consequently much lower. The total life cycle costs, therefore, may be lower and the total risk to the organization through purchasing the more expensive piping system therefore represents a good asset management decision.

A poor asset management decision might be to reduce the frequency of maintenance activity on an asset without appreciating the full impact of doing so.

Whilst there may be a short term financial benefit, the long term cost to the organization, if the asset prematurely fails, might substantially outweigh this benefit. Of course, maintenance is recognized as a means of introducing failures, so proper investigation may prove that reducing maintenance frequency is a net benefit to the organization!

3.2   What Asset Management is and isn't

3.2.1 Asset Management

i.   **Is** a recognition that assets have a life cycle
ii.   **Is** an approach that looks to get the best out of the assets for the benefit of the organization and/or its stakeholders
iii.   **Is** about understanding and managing the risk associated with owning assets. One of the challenges with managing an asset is that it is not sentient. It does not keep management edicts. It does not respond to the economy or politics. But it does respond to how it is treated and used. This creates a challenge for management. How do you get the right behavior from an entity that won't listen?

Asset Management:

i.   **Is not** just about maintenance. Maintenance is part of the stewardship of assets, but so is design, procurement, installation, commissioning, operation, etc.
ii.   **Is not** a substitute for quality management. Asset Management, like other management processes, should be subject to scrutiny through a quality process to ensure rigour.

iii. **Is not** just for engineers. Everyone working in a company that owns or operates asset should be interested. This includes those working in procurement, finance, personnel, service, planning, design, operations, administration, and leadership, marketing and sales.

3.2.2 Importance of Asset Management

Asset Management is important because it can help organizations to:

i. **Reduce** the total **costs of operating** their assets
ii. **Reduce** the **capital costs** of investing in the asset base
iii. **Improve** the **operating performance** of their assets (reduce failure rates, increase availability, etc)
iv. **Reduce** the potential **health impacts** of operating the assets
v. **Reduce** the **safety risks** of operating the assets
vi. **Minimize** the **environmental impact** of operating the assets
vii. Maintain and **improve** the **reputation** of the organization
viii. **Improve** the **regulatory performance** of the organization
ix. **Reduce legal risks** associated with operating assets

The key to good Asset Management is that it **OPTIMISES** these benefits. That means that asset management takes all of the above into account and determines the best blend of activity to achieve the best balance for all of the above for the benefit of the organization.

Asset Management is **explicitly focused** on **helping organizations to achieve their defined objectives and to determine the optimal blend of activities based on these objectives.**

3.2.3 Functions of Asset Manager

There are seven key activities that asset managers get involved in. It is important to understand that all of these activities overlap:

i. **Developing Policy**
   The Asset Management Policy is the link between the Organizational Plan (that is the top level 'business plan' in a company) and the Asset Management Strategy. It is typically a set of principles or guidelines to steer Asset Management activity to achieve the organization's objectives. It specifically covers the 'what' and the 'why'.

ii.   Developing Strategy

The Asset Management Strategy directs the organization's Asset Management activity; it will determine the high level Asset Management objectives that are needed from the activity to deliver the organization's objectives; it will define the approach to planning that will be taken.

iii.   Asset Management Planning

Asset Management Planning looks at considering all the options for activities and investments going forward and then putting together a set of plans which describe what will be done when and by whom. The asset manager ensures that the plan delivers what is required of it by the strategy.

iv.   Delivering the Plans

This is the bit where work is actually done on the assets, whether assessing or monitoring them, maintaining or repairing them, refurbishing or replacing them. This activity clearly needs to include the appropriate controls to ensure the work is done efficiently and that information gathered is fed back into the strategy and planning activities.

v.   Developing People

This activity is specifically about developing the skills and competences of people to better deliver Asset Management activities. It spans from the board room to the tool box and also through the supply chain. As well as individual skills, it looks at the culture within an organization and how change can be managed to achieve optimal results for that organization.

vi.   Managing Risk

Understanding risk is a critical concept in Asset Management and is a key function and area of competence. Its focus is on being able to assess the risk of action or inaction on the performance of assets in the context of the organization's corporate objectives.

vii.   Managing Asset Information

Collecting and collating the right information to inform Asset Management decisions is crucial to achieving Asset Management success. Too much data confuses the picture and costs money to collect and too little data results in decisions made in the dark (or at best the twilight!).

Ensuring that the right people have the right information to make the best decisions is a key.

4.0   SUMMARY

In this unit, we examined asset management as well as its purpose. The functions of an asset manager are equally given adequate attention.

5.0   CONCLUSION

Asset Management is explicitly focused on helping organizations to achieve their defined objectives and to determine the optimal blend of activities based on various objectives discussed in this unit.

SELF-ASSESSMENT EXERCISE

1.   What is asset management?
2.   What are the importance asset management?

6.0   TUTOR-MARKED ASSIGNMENT

Discuss the functions of an asset manager.

UNIT 4   ENTERPRISE MANAGEMENT

CONTENTS

1.0   Introduction
2.0   Objectives
3.0   Main Content
    3.1   Business in Contemporary Society
    3.2   Cycle of business
    3.3   Forms of Business Organization
4.0   Conclusion
5.0   Summary
6.0   Tutor-Marked Assignment

1.0   INTRODUCTION

The management of enterprise in this contemporary time cannot be over-emphasized. However, understanding the various forms of business organization is a perquisite. This unit therefore examines the different business organizations we have – from sole proprietorship to partnership to limited companies. Their merits and demerits are given considerations.

2.0   OBJECTIVES

At the end of the unit, you should be able to:

- describe business in contemporary society
- state the cycle of business
- state the various forms of business organization.

3.0   MAIN CONTENT

3.1   Business in Contemporary Society

Everyone in our society has 'wants'. Some wants are for things like food, clothing and shelter while others are for entertainment, leisure, travel and so on. Taking everybody in society together, there are millions of wants. To satisfy these wants we make use of (or consume) goods and services. If suitable goods and services were not available, we would not be able to satisfy our wants. This is why business activity is important: because it is through business activity that goods and services are provided.

A definition of business activity is any kind of activity that results in the provision of goods and services which satisfy human wants.

Goods are tangible while services are intangible. Goods sold to the general public are often referred to as consumer goods. Consumer goods may be classified as **durable goods** like cars, washing machines, or personal computers; or **non-durable goods** like sweets, drinks, newspapers. Durable goods can be used regularly over a long period of time while non-durable goods are consumed over a short period, usually soon after they are bought. Examples of services are going to the hairdresser, being served in a restaurant, or visiting a doctor.

Goods and services can be described as the **outputs** of business activity. In order to produce these outputs, business makes use of **resources**, also called factors of production.

Factors of production are classified into four categories:

i.   **land** (i.e. all natural resources, from mineral deposits to the site of a factory)
ii. **labour** (i.e. all human resources)
iii. **capital** (i.e. all resources which have been made by labour, such as machinery and other equipment)
iv. **enterprise** (i.e. organizing the other factors of production and taking the risk of producing goods or services in advance of them being sold).

In summary, then, business activity involves using resources to produce goods and services which people require in order to satisfy their wants.

Business activity can be described as 'wealth-creating'. This is because the term 'wealth' is used to refer to the amount of goods and services, or output available – the more goods and services that exist the greater the amount of wealth. In this sense, then, wealth is not money as such but the total of goods and services which can be given a monetary value.

Finally, goods and services are sold in **markets**. These exist where goods and services are exchanged between consumers and producers. Examples of markets are the housing market, the market for snack foods, and the financial services market.

3.2   Cycle of business

This phrase is sometimes used to describe the various stages of business activity. These stages can be shown as follows:

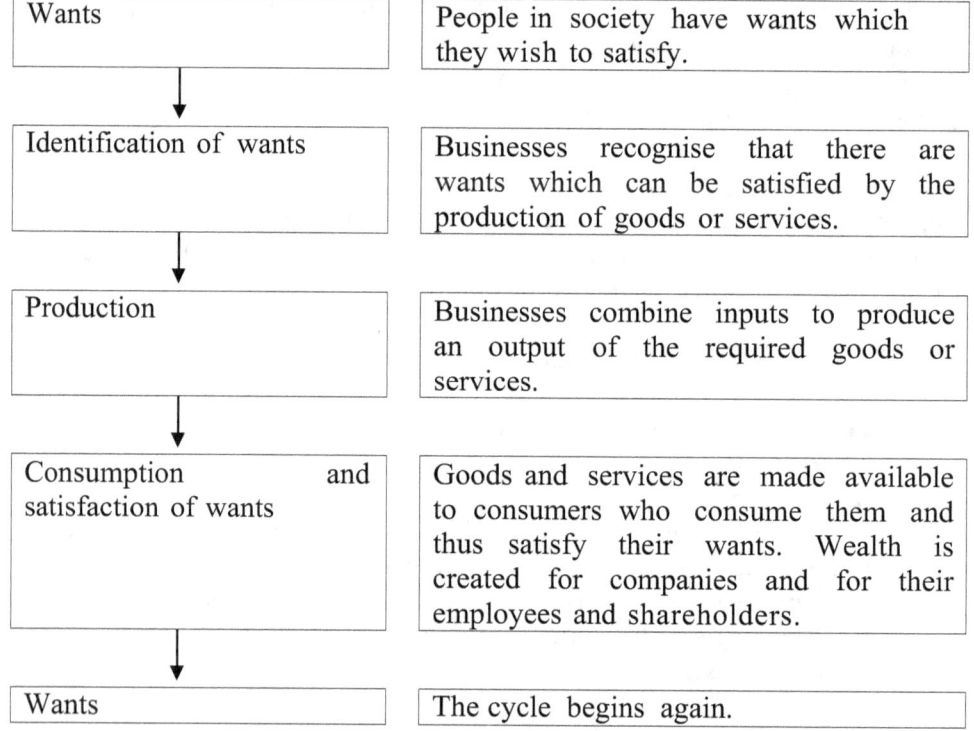

Wants	People in society have wants which they wish to satisfy.
Identification of wants	Businesses recognise that there are wants which can be satisfied by the production of goods or services.
Production	Businesses combine inputs to produce an output of the required goods or services.
Consumption and satisfaction of wants	Goods and services are made available to consumers who consume them and thus satisfy their wants. Wealth is created for companies and for their employees and shareholders.
Wants	The cycle begins again.

3.3   Forms of Business Organization

After identifying the business in any field e.g., Insurance, it is necessary then to have a legal entity to be known in the society. The legal entity can be in any form of a business organization.

The various forms of organization are as follows:

1)   Sole proprietorship
2)   Partnership

3)   Co-operative Society
4)   Joint Stock Company (Private and Public)

3.3.1 Sole proprietor (sole trader)

Definition: an organization which is owned and run by a single individual. The owner provides the capital (the money required to start up the business).

The sole proprietorship is a form of business that is owned, managed and controlled by an individual. He has to arrange capital for the business and he alone is responsible for its management. He is therefore, entitled to the profits and has to bear the loss of business, however, he can take the help of his family members and also make use of the services of others such as a manager and other employees.

Advantages
i.   It is easy and cheap to set up as there are no legal formalities.
ii.   The owner has complete control and takes all decisions.
iii.   There is no division of profits.
iv.   Profits are kept by the owner.

Disadvantages
i.   It can be difficult to raise finance – the sole trader may have to rely on savings or finance from relatives to get started. Banks may provide finance but may charge higher rates of interest if they are willing to lend at all.
ii.   The proprietor is solely responsible for all the financial commitments. A sole trader has 'unlimited liability', which means that, should the business fail, the owner can be held personally responsible for its debts, even to the extent of having to sell everything they own. This might mean s/he could face bankruptcy if the business fails.
iii.   There is no one with whom to share the responsibilities of running the business – many sole traders work long hours with few holidays.

Examples: small newsagents, hairdressers, plumbers.

3.3.2 Partnership

Definition: a business which is formed by two or more people on the basis of a *partnership agreement.* The partners provide the capital to start the business.

The maximum number of partners allowed by law is 20, although an exception is made for some professions such as solicitors and accountants.

Partnerships in general have unlimited liability, although the Limited Partnership Act allows *sleeping partners* – those who merely contribute finance but do not take an active part in running the business – to enjoy limited liability.

Advantages
i.   The responsibilities of ownership can be shared.
ii.   Partners can specialize in their areas of expertise.
iii.   A larger amount of capital is available.

Disadvantages
i.   All partners except 'sleeping partners' have unlimited liability for the debts of the business. Thus some partners may end up paying for mistakes made by other partners.
ii.   There may be conflict between partners over matters such as whom to employ or whether to borrow money.
iii.   There may be a lack of continuity as partner's change.
iv.   Profits have to be shared.

3.3.3 Limited Company (Ltd Co)

The capital of a company is divided into shares – each member or shareholder owns a number of these shares. The company must have a minimum of 2 shareholders. Limited companies are run by a Board of Directors who are appointed by the shareholders. Limited Companies must complete 2 documents – the *Memorandum of Association* and *Articles of Association* – these set out the aims of the business and how it will be run and financed. The company must register with the Registrar of Companies and must:

i.   A private limited company (Ltd) is not allowed to offer shares to the public through the stock exchange.
ii.   Limited liability means investors (shareholders) do not risk

personal bankruptcy. A company is treated as a separate legal entity from its owners. Thus a company can own assets, employ people and be sued. Just as one person cannot be held responsible for the debts of another, so owners of a company cannot be forced to pay the company's debts.

iii. A measure of privacy can still be retained – private companies are not obliged to publish their annual reports or issue a prospectus to members of the public if requested.

Public Limited Company (PLC)

A PLC is generally a large company – with a minimum share capital as stated in law. The shares of PLCs can be bought and sold on the stock exchange – large amounts of capital can be raised by selling shares to investors. PLCs must also complete a *Memorandum of Association* and *Articles of Association.* PLCs must also be registered with the Registrar of Companies and:

i. Shareholders are entitled to limited liability.

ii. Knowledge that shares in public limited companies can be resold on the Stock Exchange if required encourages people to invest.

iii. Huge sums of capital can be raised from individuals and institutional investors such as Pension Funds and Insurance Companies.

iv. All the above mean financial stability for the company which enable it to develop and expand.

Disadvantages

i. Members of the public can examine financial information about companies which is lodged with the Registrar of Companies. PLCs have to make more information available to the public than private limited companies – for example, they must publish Annual Reports.

ii. PLCs may grow so large that they become inflexible and difficult to manage effectively.

iii. In very large companies, employees may feel out of touch ('alienated') from those at the top and it may be difficult to take a personal approach to customer service.

iv. The legal procedures necessary to set up companies, especially PLCs, can be very costly.

Many large PLCs operate as **multi-national corporations**. Multi-national corporations have branches (called *subsidiaries*) in more than one country. Many companies establish sales outlets for their products in various countries. However, the distinguishing feature of an MNC is that it sets up **production facilities** in more than one country. British multi-nationals include BP and ICI. MNCs are major employers in many countries.

Reasons for establishing MNCs:

i.   to increase market share
ii.   to secure cheaper premises and labour
iii. to avoid or minimize the amount of tax which has to be paid
iv.   to take advantage of government grants available
v.   to save on costs of transporting goods to the market place
vi.   to avoid trade barriers like the EU Common External Tariff
vii. to enable their products to be sold globally without having to rely on other companies to sell them in some areas, under licence.

Disadvantages of MNCs for the host country:

i.   They can be very powerful – some of them earn more than some small countries in the course of a year – and can therefore exert quite a strong influence on the governments of host countries – for example, by threatening to close down their operations there.
ii.   They can be accused of exploiting labour in low wage countries.
iii. They may use up non-renewable resources in the host country.
iv.   Because they are so powerful and able to take advantage of economies of scale, they may force local firms out of business.
v.   Profits go back to the parent company – in which ever country it has its headquarters.
vi.   All the major functions tend to remain at headquarters so that, in times of difficulty, it is relatively easy for the MNC to close down a subsidiary causing many job losses.

4.0   CONCLUSION

In summary, business activity involves using resources to produce goods and services which people require in order to satisfy their wants. The management of enterprise in this contemporary time cannot be over-emphasized. However, understanding the various forms of business organization is a perquisite.

5.0   SUMMARY

This unit examined the various forms of business organization – sole proprietorship, partnership and limited companies. Their advantages and disadvantages were treated among others.

SELF-ASSESSMENT EXERCISE

1.   Everyone in our society has 'wants'. Discuss the role of business organizations.
2.   Mention the cycle of business.

6.0   TUTOR-MARKED ASSIGNEMENT

Discuss the various forms of business organization

MODULE 5

UNIT 1   FINANCIAL MANAGEMENT RISK

CONTENTS

1.0   Introduction
2.0   Objectives
3.0   Main Content
        3.1   Risk
        3.2   Risk Management
        3.3   Risk Management Process
4.0   Conclusion
5.0   Summary
6.0   Tutor-Marked Assignment

1.0   INTRODUCTION

Risk management is an activity which integrates recognition of risk, risk assessment, developing strategies to manage it, and mitigation of risk using managerial resources.

Risk management is concerned with understanding and managing the risks that an organization faces in its attempt to achieve its objectives. These risks will often represent threats to the organization – such as the risk of heavy losses or even bankruptcy. Risk management has traditionally associated itself with managing the risks of events that would damage the organization.

This unit, therefore, focuses on financial management risk.

2.0   OBJECTIVES

At the end of this unit, you should be able to:

- define risk
- describe risk management
- state the process of risk management.

3.0 MAIN CONTENT

3.1 Risk

Risk is unavoidable and present in every human situation. It is present in daily lives, public and private sector organizations. Depending on the context (insurance, stakeholder, technical causes), there are many accepted definitions of risk in use.

The common concept in all definitions is uncertainty of outcomes. Where they differ is in how they characterize outcomes. Some describe risk as having only adverse consequences, while others are neutral.

One description of risk is the following: risk refers to the uncertainty that surrounds future events and outcomes. It is the expression of the likelihood and impact of an event with the potential to influence the achievement of an organization's objectives.

3.2 Risk Management

As with the definition of risk, there are equally many accepted definitions of risk management in use. Some describe risk management as the decision-making process, excluding the identification and assessment of risk, whereas others describe risk management as the complete process, including risk identification, assessment and decisions around risk issues.

One well accepted description of risk management is the following: risk management is a systematic approach to setting the best course of action under uncertainty by identifying, assessing, understanding, acting on and communicating risk issues.

SELF-ASSESSMENT EXERCISE

Define risk and risk management.

3.3 Risk Management Process

The different tasks of risk management are structured in a process of chronological phases. Although different researchers and authors alike define the phases similarly, the definitions to be found in the literature differ in the way the tasks are ordered into the phases. Furthermore, the wording differs also, although the tasks to be done in the process stay the same. Therefore, the difference in the definitions does not change the general steps of the process, which are visualized in figure 2.

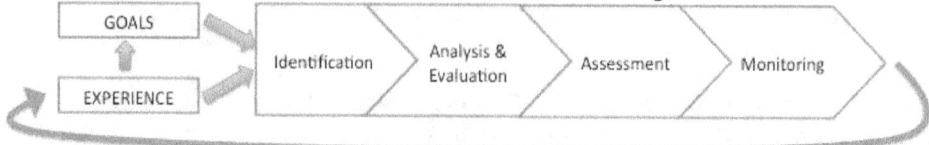

Figure 2: *Risk Management Process*

The process of risk management starts with the identification of risks. This is followed by the analysis and evaluation of risks. After that, in the risk assessment, the best ways to handle the identified risks and how this handling can be included into daily business are evaluated. The final step of the process is the risk monitoring, which becomes part of the daily business until the process is started again from the beginning.

These phases are presented in detail in the following sub-units.

3.3.1 Risk identification

The first phase is risk identification. The aim of this phase to identify all risks which could interrupt or damage the business development. The risks that should be identified can either have a negative impact on the balance sheet, the financial statement or the cash flow situation of the company and therefore also on its' development. This identification is of great importance as only identified risks can be handled successfully in the next steps of risk management.

The uncertainties of the company and critical factors of the business can be identified by checking the business processes with regard to their risk potential.

3.3.2 Risk analysis and evaluation

Once the risks are identified, they need to be analyzed and evaluated. The separation of the first and the second phase of the risk management process is not clear, as they are directly based upon each other. In defining a process or position as a risk can already be viewed as an analysis or evaluation. However, this does not change the process, where after the identification the risks are categorized and then evaluated.

The aim of the risk evaluation is to determine the degree of the identified risks and quantify their financial impact on the company. It is therefore necessary to analyze in which way the risk could affect the business.

In order to get a better overview, the identified risks are first clustered or categorized based on the field of risk, for example whether it is market or financial risks. More specifically the source of origin determined by the single risk factors of the risk fields can be used. The clustering allows for a company to later analyze whether some of the risks are related and whether some of them offset each other (e.g. in and outflows in a foreign currency). Furthermore, the clustering will assist to identify the main risks of business, which is of help for future analysis and focus of risk management.

Next the influence of the different risks and their potential harm to the company needs to be evaluated. This will require an identification of the costs to the company in case the risk occurs as well as the probability of occurrence. With help of those values the expected damages of the risk positions can be calculated and the single risks can be evaluated.

3.3.3 Risk assessment

According to the risk willingness, measures to handle the risk will be chosen in the third phase. Those measures range from risk avoidance or prevention, over risk reduction, to transfer of risks and finally acceptance of the risk.

A simple measure to handle an identified risk position is to decide to avoid the risk. However, the company has to accept that avoiding single risks eliminates besides the risk also all activities and chances connected with it. The abandonment of possible gains of risky activities is not always possible and also not aimed when doing business.

3.3.4 Risk monitoring

At the last phase of the risk management process it should be checked with a risk monitoring whether the risk identification, evaluation and assessment have been successful. This phase is crucial for taking appropriate measures in time in case deviations between the actual and planned risk situation are identified. The monitoring should therefore include developments of the risk positions and measures to control them. Moreover, the overall risk situation of the company should be compared to the plan and the risk strategy and deviations should be documented. When identifying differences, the risk management process should be started all over again. In iterative learning the next circle of the risk management process will start.

4.0   SUMMARY

In this unit, we examined the meaning of risk and risk management. The process of risk management was also given adequate consideration.

5.0   CONCLUSION

The underlying premise of risk management is that every entity exists to provide value for its stakeholders. All entities face uncertainty, and the challenge for management is to determine how much uncertainty to accept as it strives to grow stakeholder value. Uncertainty presents both risk and opportunity, with the potential to erode or enhance value. Risk management enables management to effectively deal with uncertainty and associated risk and opportunity thereby enhancing the capacity to build value.

The real benefits of financial risk management must be understood in terms of what it tries to avoid than what it tries to do. By preventing undesirable situations, it ensures that management is not distracted from its core purpose of running its business efficiently. Financial risk management aims to maximize shareholders' wealth.

Self-Assessment Exercise

Define risk and risk management.

6.0   TUTOR-MARKED ASSIGNMENTS

State the process of risk management

UNIT 2   METHODS OF AVOIDING FINANCIAL RISKS

CONTENTS

1.0   INTRODUCTION

In previous unit, we considered financial management risk. However, in this unit, we shall examine financial risk and its various types which organizations face and the techniques they can use to reduce or eliminate them.

2.0   OBJECTIVES

At the end of this unit, you should be able to:

- define financial risk
- state the different types of financial risk
- list the reasons for managing financial risk
- analyze the various ways of dealing with financial risk

3.0   MAIN CONTENT

3.1   Financial Risk

Financial risks create the possibility of losses arising from the failure to achieve a financial objective. The risk reflects uncertainty about foreign exchange rates, interest rates, commodity prices, equity prices, credit quality, liquidity, and an organization's access to financing. These financial risks are not necessarily independent of each other. For instance, exchange rates and interest rates are often strongly linked, and this interdependence should be recognized when managers are designing risk management systems.

These financial risks relate to the financial operation of a business – in essence, the risk of financial loss (and in some cases, financial gain) – and take many different forms. These include currency risks, interest rate risks, credit risks, liquidity risks, cash flow risk, and financing risks (explanations are given in subsequent sections). The importance of these risks will vary from one organization to another. A firm that operates internationally will be more exposed to currency risks than a firm that operates only domestically; a bank will typically be more exposed to credit risks than most other firms, and so forth.

3.2   Different types of financial risk

Financial risks can be subdivided into distinct categories; a convenient classification is discussed as follows.

(a)   *Market risks:* These are the financial risks that arise because of possible losses due to changes in future market prices or rates. The price changes will often relate to interest or foreign exchange rate movements, but also include the price of basic commodities that are vital to the business.

(b)   *Credit risks:* Financial risks associated with the possibility of default by counter-party. Credit risks typically arise because customers fail to pay for goods supplied on credit.

Credit risk exposure increases substantially when a firm depends heavily upon a small number of large customers who have been granted access to a significant amount of credit. The significance of credit risk varies between sectors, and is high in the area of financial services, where short- and long-term lending are fundamental to the business.

A firm can also be exposed to the credit risks of other firms with which it is heavily connected. For example, a firm may suffer losses if a key supplier or partner in a joint venture has difficulty accessing credit to continue trading.

(c)   *Financing, liquidity and cash flow risks:* Financing risks affect an organization's ability to obtain ongoing financing. An obvious example is the dependence of a firm on its access to credit from its bank. Liquidity risk refers to uncertainty regarding the ability of a firm to unwind a position at little or no cost, and also relates to the availability of sufficient funds to meet financial commitments when

they fall due. Cash flow risks relate to the volatility of the firm's day-to-day operating cash flow.

3.3 Why Manage Financial Risks?

Firms can benefit from financial risk management in many different ways, but perhaps the most important benefit is to protect the firm's ability to attend to its core business and achieve its strategic objectives. By making stakeholders more secure, a good risk management policy helps encourage equity investors, creditors, managers, workers, suppliers, and customers to remain loyal to the business. In short, the firm's goodwill is strengthened in all manner of diverse and mutually reinforcing ways. This leads to a wide variety of ancillary benefits:

a.   The firm's reputation or 'brand' is enhanced, as the firm is seen as successful and its management is viewed as both competent and credible.

b.   Risk management can reduce earnings volatility, which helps to make financial statements and dividend announcements more relevant and reliable.

c.   Greater earnings stability also tends to reduce average tax liabilities.

d.   Risk management can protect a firm's cash flows.

e.   Some commentators suggest that risk management may reduce the cost of capital, therefore raising the potential economic value added for a business.

f.   The firm is better placed to exploit opportunities (such as opportunities to invest) through an improved credit rating and more secure access to financing.

g.   The firm is in a stronger position to deal with merger and acquisitions issues. It is also in a stronger position to take over other firms and to fight off hostile takeover bids

h.   The firm has a better managed supply chain, and a more stable customer base.

These benefits show that it is difficult to separate the effects of financial risk management from the broader activities of the business. It is therefore important to ensure that all parties within the organization recognize and understand how they might create or control financial risks. For example, staff in the marketing department might be trained on how to reduce financial risks through their approach to pricing and customer vetting. Similarly, buying policies can create financial risks, for example, by creating an exposure to exchange rate movements. Consequently, it is important to establish an integrated framework for managing all financial risks.

3.4 Ways of Dealing with Financial Risk

We can deal with financial risks in various ways:

i.   *Avoidance:* The firm can avoid holding financial assets or liabilities whose values are uncertain.

ii.   *Loss Control:* When risks cannot be avoided, efforts can be made to limit the loss.

iii. *Diversification:* Instead of concentrating assets in one place, the firm can distribute them across several locations or markets.

iv.   *Transfer:* The risk can be eliminated by transferring the asset/liability to another party. Alternatively, the asset/liability can be retained by the company but the risk can be transferred. Or the company may retain the risk but in the event of a loss, a third party assumes the liability.

4.0   CONCLUSION

In this unit, we examined the meaning of risk and risk management. The process of risk management was also given adequate consideration.

5.0   SUMMARY

A firm is exposed to financial risk when the value of its assets, liabilities, operating incomes and cash flows are affected by changes in financial parameters such as interest rates, exchange rates, stock indices, etc. Financial risk management aims to reduce the volatility of earnings and boost the confidence of investors in the company.

6.0   TUTOR-MARKED ASSIGNMENT

What are the different ways of dealing with financial risks?

UNIT 3   BANKING SYSTEM

CONTENTS

1.0   INTRODUCTION

The Nigerian banking system is a subset of the Nigerian Financial system. The financial system is the totality of institutions, bodies, rules and regulations governing the flow of financial resources within the economy.
In this unit, we therefore examine the financial system vis-à-vis the banking system in Nigeria.

2.0   OBJECTIVES

At the end of this unit, you should be able to:

- Discuss the financial system.
- Explain the evolution of the financial system.
- Explain the component of the Nigerian financial system.
- Discuss the central bank, commercial banks and others
- State the procedures involved in establishing a bank in Nigeria.
- Distinguish between central bank and commercial bank.

3.0   Main Content

3.1   The Financial System

The financial system is the totality of institutions, bodies, rules and regulations governing the flow of financial resources within the economy. The Nigeria financial system is described as the framework of:

1.   Laws and regulations
2.   Financial institutions
3.   Practices which direct the flow of financial resources within the economy.

Broadly speaking, "A financial system consists of a network of financial links between economic units – a web of debentures and shares. The financial system is a superstructure created on the basis of the real wealth of the economy" .

The financial system itself is an omnibus term which encompasses the generality of financial intermediaries that operate in the financial sector and the institutional facilities being employed in its operational activities within the economy.

3.2   Evolution of the Financial System

The financial system as it is today developed from the effort of individuals who productively engage in trade; exchanging goods for goods in what was primordially denoted as barter. Trade by barter evolve the present financial system. The process succeeds as long as the buyer and seller of equivalent goods exist. However, with ever increasing volume of activities and the need to exchange a variety of commodities (of the seller) for a single product and vice versa, the barter system soon became not only cumbersome but also inadequate on the one hand, surplus units could not preserve their surplus in the most convenient form and on the other hand, deficit units could not obtain resource they require in the most convenient form on the other hand.

The poor performance of the barter system soon paved the way for the usage of gold as a means of exchange. As gold soon became means of exchanging good for good; the higher the quantity of gold you possess, the better your capacity to trade. Gold a commodity in itself soon became what could be exchanged for other forms of goods and services. Several values exist for several forms of gold and with these value, equivalent amount of goods and services were exchanged.

The gold system was sustained for a long period of time. In England, precious metals and coins were used almost exclusively as money until the middle of the seventeenth century. However, in 1640, Charles I appropriated £130,000 worth of gold held for merchants in the tower of London.

Thereafter, gold and silver bullion plates were kept in the strong rooms of the goldsmiths. Eventually receipts for these deposits were accepted in exchange for goods and so withdrawal of the actual gold and silver became unnecessary.

This was the origin of the bank note and paper currency which soon began forming an increasing proportion of British money. The paper from which notes are made is comparatively worthless. However people who receive note are confident that other too will accept them. **The evolution of money in its present form was the next stage and with money came the need for financial assets and claims in the form we have them today.** The creation of financial assets and claims was facilitated by the emergence of financial intermediaries, which perform the crucial function of matching the needs of surplus units with those of the deficit units. These functions were performed in the form of financial markets-notably the money market and the capital markets.

The financial institutions, consisting of the money market and the capital market stand as the major subject of financial system mostly in a developed economy where the governments play only a little role in the financial intermediation. However, in a developing nation like Nigeria, the financial system cannot function without the activities of the government, which makes for a great player in the financial system. Most times in a nation like ours, financial intermediation remains at the subsidiary level because non-financial activities are done in Cash rather than through other more articulated means which avoid the risk of Cash and the cumbersomeness of money.

In view of the foregoing, we hereby examine in seriatim, the Nigeria financial institutions – the central bank, the commercial bank, the merchant bank among others.

3.3   The Nigerian Banking System

3.3.1 The Central Bank of Nigeria (CBN)

The CBN is the apex regulatory authority of the financial system. It was established by the Central Bank of Nigeria Act of 1958 and commenced operations on 1st July 1959. Among its primary functions, the Bank promotes monetary stability and a sound financial system, and acts as banker and financial adviser to the Federal Government, as well as banker of last resort to the banks. The Bank also encourages the growth and development of financial institutions. Enabling laws made in 1991 gave the

Bank more flexibility in regulating and overseeing the banking sector and licensing finance companies, which hitherto operated outside any regulatory framework. Also it needs to be stated that in the recent years the power of the CBN have been grossly increased to enhance efficiency in the financial sector.

3.3.2 Commercial and Merchant Banks

Commercial and Merchant Banks operate under the legal framework of the Banks and other Financial Institutions (BOFI) Act 25 of 1991 (as amended).

Commercial banks perform three major functions, namely, acceptance of deposits, granting of loans and the operation of the payment and settlement mechanism. Since the Government commenced active deregulation of the economy in September 1986, the commercial banking sector has continued to witness rapid growth, especially in terms of the number of institutions and product innovations in the market.

Merchant banks take deposit and cater for the needs of corporate and institutional customers by way of providing medium and long-term loan financing and engaging in activities such as equipment leasing, loan syndication, debt factoring and project advisers to clients sourcing funds in the market. The first merchant bank in Nigeria, Nigerian Acceptance Limited (NAL), started operations in 1960.

Currently, there is a general banking operation. With this banks performs multiple operations whether commercial or merchant operation

3.3.3 Community Banks

A community bank in Nigeria is a self-sustaining financial institution owned and managed within a community to provide financial services to that community. The National Board for Community Banks (NBCB) processes applications for the establishment of community banks. The first community bank commenced operation in December 1990. Since then, NBCB has issued provisional licences to 1,366 community banks and are expected to be issued final licences by the CBN after operating for two years.

3.3.4 Differences between Central Bank and Commercial Bank

There are basic differences between the central bank and a commercial bank in terms of their structure and operations in the following ways:

i.   The central bank is the apex institution of the monetary and banking structure of the country. The commercial bank is one of the organs of the money market.

ii.   The central bank does not operate as a profit-driven institution but only implements the economic policies of the government. But the commercial bank is a profit-making institution.

iii.   The central bank is owned by the government, whereas the commercial bank is owned by private individuals as shareholders.

iv.   The central bank is a banker to the government and does not engage itself in ordinary banking activities. The commercial bank is a banker to the general public.

v.   The central bank has the monopoly of issuing currency of the country as the legal tender but the commercial bank can issue only cheques to its customers; the currency notes and coins issued by a central bank constitute legal tender. But the cheques are mere near-money.

vi.   The central bank is the banker to commercial banks. Therefore, it grants window of opportunity for credits to commercial banks in the form of rediscount facilities, keeps their cash reserves, and clears their balances in cheque settlements. On the other contrary, the commercial bank accepts deposits from the general public and grants loans and advances to the customers.

vii.   The central bank controls credit in accordance with the needs and policy of the government and the business and economy generally. The commercial bank creates credit to meet the requirements of business.

viii.   The central bank helps in establishing financial institutions so as to strengthen money and capital markets in a country. On the other hand, the commercial bank helps industries by underwriting shares and debentures, and agriculture by meeting its financial requirements through cooperatives or individually.

ix.   Every country has only one central bank with its offices at important centres in the country. On the other hand, there are many commercial banks with hundreds of branches within and outside the country.

x.   The central bank is the custodian of the foreign currencies of the country while the commercial bank is a dealer in foreign exchange in terms of buying and selling.

SELF-ASSESSMENT EXERCISES

1. What are the differences between central bank and commercial banks?
2. Discuss the evolution of the financial system.

3.3.5 Procedures for Establishing a Bank in Nigeria

1. Any person desiring to undertake banking business in Nigeria shall apply in writing to the Governor for the grant of a licence and shall accompany the application with the following:
- A feasibility report of the proposed bank;
- A draft copy of the memorandum and articles of association of the proposed bank;
- A list of the shareholders, directors and principal officers of the proposed bank and their particulars;
- The prescribed application fee and other information, documents and reports as the bank may, from time to time, specify
2. After the applicant has provided all such information, documents and reports as the bank may require the shareholders of the proposed bank to deposit with the bank a sum equal to the minimum paid-up capital that may be applicable.
3. Upon the payment of the 25billion Naira paid-up capital, the Governor may issue a license with or without conditions or refuse to issue a licence and the Governor need not give any reason for the refusal.
4. Where an application for a licence is granted, the bank shall give written notice of that fact to the applicant and the licence fee shall be paid.

SELF-ASSESSMENT EXERCISES (SAES) 2

What are the procedures for establishing a bank in Nigeria?

5.0 SUMMARY

The evolution of the Nigeria financial system and its financial institutions particularly, central bank, commercial bank, merchant bank and community bank were treated in this unit. Also, the procedures involved in establishing bank in Nigeria were considered.

4.0   CONCLUSION

The Nigerian financial system comprises of bank and non-bank financial institutions which are regulated by the Federal Ministry of Finance (FMF), Central Bank of Nigeria (CBN), Nigeria Deposit Insurance Corporation (NDIC), Securities and Exchange Commission (SEC), National Insurance Commission (NAICOM), Federal Mortgage Bank of Nigeria (FMBN), and the National Board for Community Banks.

SELF-ASSESSMENT EXERCISE

1.   What are the differences between central bank and commercial banks?
2.   Discuss the evolution of the financial system.

6.0   TUTOR-MARKED ASSIGNMENT (TMA)

The banking system is a component of the financial system. Discuss.

UNIT 4 MORTGAGE FINANCE

CONTENTS

1.0   INTRODUCTION

Mortgage or house finance has been recognized as an important, almost indispensable factor in the housing delivery system. This is because only the very few in any nation can afford to pay cash for a house. Most other people must have to finance their house through loans, personal savings, assistance from relatives or friends and gifts.

Consequent to the foregoing, we shall examine in this unit, mortgage finance as well as other related issues.

2.0   OBJECTIVES

At the end of this unit, you should be able to:

- discuss mortgage finance
- state the historical background of mortgage finance in Nigeria
- discuss the finance options for housing in Nigeria.

3.0   MAIN CONTENT

3.1   Mortgage Finance

The housing sector plays a more critical role in a nation's welfare than is always recognized, as it directly affects not only the citizenry, but also the performance of other sectors of the economy. Adequate housing provision

150

has since the early 1970s consequently engaged the attention of most countries, especially the developing nations, Nigeria inclusive, for a number of reasons. First, it is one of the three most important basic needs of mankind- the others being food and clothing. Secondly, housing is a very important durable consumer item, which impacts positively on productivity, as decent housing significantly increases worker's health and wellbeing, and consequently growth. Thirdly, it is one of the indices for measuring the standard of living of people across societies.

Housing finance constitutes one of the major pillars of housing delivery system. Indeed, without a well-organized and efficient housing finance mechanism, the goal of a housing development policy will be largely unattainable. Housing finance has been recognized as an important, almost indispensable factor in the housing delivery system. This is because only the very few in any nation can afford to pay cash for a house. Most other people must have to finance their house through loans, personal savings, assistance from relatives or friends and gifts.

3.2 An Historical Overview of Mortgage Developing Countries

Mortgage lending in developing countries prior to 1976 was largely restricted to a single public-owned housing bank, Nigeria for example, the Nigerian Building Society (NBS), and supported by some mandatory and state contributions. The NBS was created in 1956 and converted in 1976 into the Federal Mortgage Bank of Nigeria (FMBN). The FMBN mobilized some limited deposits and granted a few mortgage loans mostly to higher-income borrowers.

Decree No. 53 of 1989 authorized the licensing of Primary Mortgage Institutions (PMIs) as specialized institutions to collect households' savings and originate mortgage loans. PMIs were based on the British model of building societies and were expected to support the development of a more vibrant and competitive housing finance sector. The Ministry of Works and Housing (MWH) and the FMBN were appointed as regulators and supervisors for PMIs. However, FMBN's regulatory and supervisory responsibilities were transferred to the CBN in 1997.

A National Housing Fund (NHF) was created by Decree No. 3 of 1992 to subsidize "affordable" mortgage loans and catalyze long term funding for PMIs and is managed by the FMBN. Collections began in 1994 and it is funded by mandatory contributions from all employees of 2.5% of basic wages with the employees earning 4% per annum on this money and becoming eligible for NHF financed loans.

By this decree, banks were expected to fund the NHF in amounts equal to 10% of overall loans and advances, to be remunerated at current account interest rate plus 1% (i.e. about 5%). Life and non-life insurance companies were also to invest 20% and 10% of their premiums respectively in the NHF, remunerated at a low fixed rate of 4%. Given inflationary conditions, CBN has never applied this requirement to banks, nor have insurance companies complied with these requirements. Such rules would have contradicted the liberalization of the financial system, undermined the interest rate structure, and put at risk the development of contractual savings institutions. However, the enacted decree has not been amended and the resulting ambiguity still affects relations between FMBN (manager of the NHF), banks and insurance companies.

3.3   Financing Options for Housing in Developing Countries

There are various options of financing options of housing before the evolvement of the modern means of financing housing development in Nigeria. The two major options will be discussed accordingly:

3.3.1 Modern Financing Options

The following are some of the modern methods of finance available for housing developments and purchase in Nigeria.

(i)   **The Federal Mortgage Bank of Nigeria (FMBN)**: The FMBN commenced operation in 1978, following the promulgation of the FBMN Decree No 7 of January 1977 as a direct Federal Government intervention to accelerate its housing delivery programme. The FMBN is expected to expand and coordinate mortgage lending on a nation-wide basis, using resources from deposit mobilized and equity contributions by the Federal Government and CBN at rates of interest below the market rates. By mid-1980s, the FMBN was the only mortgage private institution in Nigeria.

(ii)   **Primary Mortgage Institutions (PMI)**: The Mortgage Institutions Decree No.53 of 1989 provided the regulatory framework for the establishment and operation of PMIs by private entrepreneurs. The FMBN was empowered to license the PMIs as second tier housing finance institutions. The PMIs were to mobilize savings from the public and grant housing loans to individual, while the FMBN mobilizes capital fund for the PMIs.

(iii)   **Personal and Family Savings**: This constitutes a major source of finance especially for individuals who wish to build their houses themselves. In this case, individuals buy land in area zoned for housing and build their own houses, while government is expected to provide infrastructure to service the houses.

(iv)   **Corporate organizations:** With the promulgation of employee Housing Scheme (Special provision) Decree 54 of 1979, any employer of up to 500 employees is expected to provide minimum of 50 housing units out of which three quarters are to be made available to non-executive staff.

SELF-ASSESSMENT EXERCISE

Discuss the financing options for housing in Nigeria.

3.4   The Mortgage Sector

3.4.1 The Federal Mortgage Bank of Nigeria (FMBN)

The FMBN took over the assets and liabilities of the Nigerian Building Society. The FMBN provides banking and advisory services, and undertakes research activities pertaining to housing. Following the adoption of the National Housing Policy in 1990, FMBN is empowered to licence and regulate primary mortgage institutions in Nigeria and act as the apex regulatory body for the Mortgage Finance Industry. The financing function of the Federal Mortgage Bank of Nigeria was carved out and transferred to the Federal Mortgage Finance, while the FMBN retains its regulatory role. FMBN is under the control of the Central Bank of Nigeria.

Federal Mortgage Bank of Nigeria (FMBN) is the first operator in Nigeria's formal institutional mortgage lending sector. The Bank thus has a history of retail, supervisory, regulatory and wholesale activities in the country's mortgage industry. The funding vehicle for its wholesale mortgage lending is the National Housing Trust Fund (NHTF). As the fallout of housing reforms started in 2002, the FMBN is now re-organized to perform mainly secondary mortgage and capital market operations.

3.4.2 Primary Mortgage Institutions (PMIs)

Primary mortgage institutions operate within the framework of Act No. 53 of 1989. PMIs mobilize savings for the development of the housing sector. Their total assets/liabilities rose to N7248.2 million in 1999. In reaction to distress in the sector, the Federal Mortgage Bank of Nigeria tightened its surveillance of the institutions by issuing "clean bill of health" to 116 mortgage institutions. The share capital requirement for new primary mortgage institutions has been raised to N20 million.

3.4.3 Concept of Primary Mortgage Market

The Primary Mortgage Market is a market where all the mortgage loans are originated. The market is a place where the mortgage originators and as well as the borrowers come together to set the mortgage deal and negotiate the terms and conditions regarding that deal. The credit unions, mortgage brokers, banks and mortgage bankers etc. all are the part of primary mortgage market. The development of a primary mortgage market depends upon macroeconomic stability of the nation. However, primary mortgage market plays an important role behind the development of a successful secondary mortgage market. The secondary mortgage market on its part, loans and servicing rights are traded between the mortgage securities, mortgage originators and investors.

4.0 SUMMARY

In this unit we examined mortgage finance and the finance options for housing in Nigeria. The Federal Mortgage Bank of Nigeria (FMBN), Primary Mortgage Institutions (PMIs) and the concept of Primary Mortgage Market were treated.

5.0   CONCLUSION

For a housing finance system to function the interconnected parts namely fund mobilization, disbursement and recoupment must be well harnessed for the system to be effective since its operation rests on mortgage finance.

SELF-ASSESSMENT EXERCISE

Discuss the financing options for housing in Nigeria.

6.0   TUTOR-MARKED ASSIGNMENT

1.   The housing sector plays a more critical role in a nation's welfare. Discuss.
2.   Trace the historical background of mortgage finance in Nigeria.

UNIT 5   CAPITAL STRUCTURE

CONTENTS

1.0   INTRODUCTION

Capital is the major part of all kinds of business activities, which are decided by the size, and nature of the business concern. Capital may be raised with the help of various sources. If the company maintains proper and adequate level of capital, it will earn high profit and they can provide more dividends to its shareholders.

In light of the above, this unit looks at capital structure of an organization as well as its forms.

2.0   OBJECTIVES

At the end of this unit, you should be able to:

- define capital structure
- discuss the objectives of capital structure
- state the forms of capital structure
- mention the factors determining capital structure
- explain the different capital structure theories.

3.0   MAIN CONTENT

3.1   Meaning of Capital Structure

Capital structure refers to the kinds of securities and the proportionate amounts that make up capitalization. It is the mix of different sources of long-term sources such as equity shares, preference shares, debentures, long-term loans and retained earnings.

The term capital structure refers to the relationship between the various long-term sources financing such as equity capital, preference share capital and debt capital. Deciding the suitable capital structure is the important decision of the financial management because it is closely related to the value of the firm.

Capital structure is the permanent financing of the company represented primarily by long-term debt and equity.

3.2   Optimum Capital Structure

Optimum capital structure is the capital structure at which the weighted average cost of capital is minimum and thereby the value of the firm is maximum.

Optimum capital structure may be defined as the capital structure or combination of debt and equity that leads to the maximum value of the firm.

3.3   Objectives of Capital Structure

Decision of capital structure aims at the following two important objectives:

1.   Maximize the value of the firm.
2.   Minimize the overall cost of capital.

3.4   Forms of Capital Structure

Capital structure pattern varies from company to company and the availability of finance.

Normally the following forms of capital structure are popular in practice:

i.   Equity shares only.
ii.   Equity and preference shares only.
iii. Equity and Debentures only.
iv.   Equity shares, preference shares and debentures.

3.5   Factors Determining Capital Structure

The following factors are considered while deciding the capital structure of the firm:

1.   **Leverage**
      It is the basic and important factor, which affect the capital structure. It uses the fixed cost financing such as debt, equity and preference share capital. It is closely related to the overall cost of capital.
2.   **Cost of Capital**
      Cost of capital constitutes the major part for deciding the capital structure of a firm.
      Normally long-term finance such as equity and debt consist of fixed cost while mobilization.
      When the cost of capital increases, value of the firm will also decrease. Hence the firm must take careful steps to reduce the cost of capital.
(a)   **Nature of the business:** Use of fixed interest/dividend bearing finance depends upon the nature of the business. If the business consists of long period of operation, it will apply for equity than debt, and it will reduce the cost of capital.
(b)   **Size of the company:** It also affects the capital structure of a firm. If the firm belongs to large scale, it can manage the financial requirements with the help of internal sources. But if it is small size, they will go for external finance. It consists of high cost of capital.
(c)   **Legal requirements:** Legal requirements are also one of the considerations while dividing the capital structure of a firm. For example, banking companies are restricted to raise funds from some sources.
(d)   **Requirement of investors:** In order to collect funds from different type of investors, it will be appropriate for the companies to issue different sources of securities.

3.   Government policy
Promoter contribution is fixed by the company Act. It restricts to mobilize large, long term funds from external sources. Hence the company must consider government policy regarding the capital structure.

3.6   Capital Structure Theories

Capital structure is the major part of the firm's financial decision which affects the value of the firm and it leads to change EBIT and market value of the shares. There is a relationship among the capital structure, cost of capital and value of the firm. The aim of effective capital structure is to maximize the value of the firm and to reduce the cost of capital.

There are two major theories explaining the relationship between capital structure, cost of capital and value of the firm.

3.7   Capital Structure Theories

1.   Modern Approach
2.   Traditional Approach
3.   Net Income Approach
4.   Net Operating Income Approach
5.   Modigliani-Miller Approach

(a)   Traditional Approach
It is the mix of Net Income approach and Net Operating Income approach. Hence, it is also called as intermediate approach. According to the traditional approach, mix of debt and equity capital can increase the value of the firm by reducing overall cost of capital up to certain level of debt. Traditional approach states that the K_o decreases only within the responsible limit of financial leverage and when reaching the minimum level, it starts increasing with financial leverage.

Assumptions
Capital structure theories are based on certain assumption to analysis in a single and convenient manner:

a.   There are only two sources of funds used by a firm; debt and shares.
b.   The firm pays 100% of its earning as dividend.
c.   The total assets are given and do not change.
d.   The total finance remains constant.
e.   The operating profits (EBIT) are not expected to grow.

f.   The business risk remains constant.
g.   The firm has a perpetual life.
h.   The investors behave rationally.

Illustration 1

ABC Ltd., needs $30,000,000 for the installation of a new factory. The new factory expects to yield annual earnings before interest and tax (EBIT) of $5,000,000. In choosing a financial plan, ABC Ltd., has an objective of maximizing earnings per share (EPS). The company proposes to issuing ordinary shares and raising debit of $3,000,000 and $10,000,000 of $ 15,000,000. The current market price per share is $250 and is expected to drop to $200 if the funds are borrowed in excess of $12,000,000. Funds can be raised at the following rates:

i.   up to $3,000,000 at 8%
ii. over $3,000,000 to $15,000,000 at 10%
iii. over $15,000,000 at 15%
     Assuming a tax rate of 50% advise the company.

Solution

Earnings Before Interest and Tax (BIT) less Interest Earnings Before Tax less: Tax@50%.

Alternatives		
I **(N3,000,000 debt)**	**II** **($10,000,000 debt)**	**III** **($15,000,000 debt)**
5,000,000	5,000,000	5,000,000
24,000	1,000,000	2,250,000
4,760,000	4,000,000	2,750,000
2,380,000	2,000,000	1,370,500
2,380,000	2,000,000	1,370,500
27,000,000	20,000,000	15,000,000
250	250	200
10,800	8,000	7,500
2,3800,000	2,000,000	1,370,500
No. of shares **10,800**	**8,000**	**7,500**
Earnings per share **22.03**	**25**	**18.33**

The secure alternative which gives the highest earnings per share is the best. Therefore the company is advised to revise $10,000,000 through debt amount $20,000,000 through ordinary shares.

(b)   Net Income (NI) Approach

Net income approach suggested by the Durand: According to this approach, the capital structure decision is relevant to the valuation of the firm. In other words, a change in the capital structure leads to a corresponding change in the overall cost of capital as well as the total value of the firm.

According to this approach, use more debt finance to reduce the overall cost of capital and increase the value of firm.

Net income approach is based on the following three important assumptions:

1.   There are no corporate taxes.
2.   The cost debt is less than the cost of equity.
3.   The use of debt does not change the risk perception of the investor.

(c)   Net Operating Income (NOI) Approach

Another modern theory of capital structure suggested by **Durand**: This is just the opposite of the Net Income approach. According to this approach, Capital Structure decision is irrelevant to the valuation of the firm. The market value of the firm is not at all affected by the capital structure changes.

According to this approach, the change in capital structure will not lead to any change in the total value of the firm and market price of shares as well as the overall cost of capital.

NI approach is based on the following important assumptions;

i.   The overall cost of capital remains constant;
ii.   There are no corporate taxes;
iii.   The market capitalizes the value of the firm as a whole;

(d)   Modigliani and Miller Approach

Modigliani and Miller approach states that the financing decision of a firm does not affect the market value of a firm in a perfect capital market. In other words MM approach maintains that the average cost of capital does not change with change in the debt weighted equity mix or capital structures of the firm.

Modigliani and Miller approach is based on the following important assumptions:

i.   There is a perfect capital market.
ii. There are no retained earnings.
iii. There are no corporate taxes.
iv. The investors act rationally.
v.   The dividend payout ratio is 100%.
vi. The business consists of the same level of business risk.

Value of the firm can be calculated with the help of the following formula:

$$\frac{EBIT}{K_o} (1-t)$$

Where:
EBIT = Earnings before interest and tax
K_o = Overall cost of capital
t = Tax rate

Illustration 2
There are two firms 'A' and 'B' which are exactly identical except that A does not use any debt in its financing, while B has $2,500,000, 6% Debentures in its financing. Both the firms have earnings before interest and tax of $75,000 and the equity capitalization rate is 10%. Assuming the corporation tax is 50%, calculate the value of the firm.

Solution
The market value of firm A which does not use any debt.

$$Vu = \frac{EBIT}{K_o} (1-t)$$

$$= \frac{75,000}{10/100}$$

$= 75,000 \times 100/10$
$= \$ 7,500,000$

The market value of firm B which uses debt financing of $ 2,500,000 Vt=
Vu + t
Vu = 7,500,000, t = 50% of $ 2,500,000
= 7,500,000 + 1,250,000
= $8,750,000

4.0   SUMMARY

In this unit we examined mortgage finance and the finance options for housing in Nigeria. The Federal Mortgage Bank of Nigeria (FMBN),

Primary Mortgage Institutions (PMIs) and the concept of Primary Mortgage Market were treated.

5.0   CONCLUSION

Capital structure refers to the kinds of securities and the proportionate amounts that make up capitalization. Capital structure is the permanent financing of the company represented primarily by long-term debt and equity. Capital structure pattern varies from company to company and the availability of finance.

6.0   TUTOR-MARKED ASSIGNMENT

1.   Define capital structure.
2.   What is optimum capital structure?
3.   Discuss the various factors affecting the capital structure.
4.   Explain the capital structure theories.
5.   XYZ Ltd., expects a net income of $1,500,000. The company has 10% of 5,000,000 Debentures. The equity capitalization rate of the company is 10%.
(a)   Calculate the value of the firm and overall capitalization rate according to the net income approach (ignoring income tax).
(b)   If the debenture debt is increased to $ 7,500,000 and interest of debt is change to 9%. What is the value of the firm and overall capitalization rate?